GW00392887

SILVOGRAPH

SILVOGRAPH

Arthur Cheetham (1865–1937)
Pioneer Film-maker

Philip Lloyd

First published in 2018

ISBN: 978-1-84524-272-5

Cover design: Eleri Owen
Cover illustrations: Cheetham's Manchester cinema, Cheetham and his wife at son
Gustavus's wedding and a diagram from a Lumière catalogue showing two types of
film perforation.

Published by Gwasg Carreg Gwalch,
12 Iard yr Orsaf, Llanrwst, Wales LL26 0EH
tel: 01492 642031
email: books@carreg-gwalch.cymru
website: www.carreg-gwalch.cymru

Dedicated to the memory of David Berry, film historian

Contents

Introduction

Arthur Cheetham is associated mainly with the north Wales seaside resort of Rhyl, which has been attracting holidaymakers since the 1820s. When he and his wife arrived there in 1889, the town's population was approaching 6,000. Although he is remembered chiefly as a film-maker, his business interests were diverse. As a phrenologist he would give lectures and demonstrations on Rhyl beach in the holiday season and provide 'character delineations' at his nearby premises. As a medical electrician he offered treatment for a variety of ailments with his electro-curative battery. He was also a printer, a publisher, a photographer and an electrician.

In his magisterial *Wales and Cinema, the First Hundred Years* David Berry maintains that Cheetham retains a secure place in any history – as the first film-maker operating in Wales and the first to shoot events specifically to be screened in his own shows. Productive between 1898 and 1912, he shot at least 47 films, depicting aspects of contemporary entertainment, sport, industry, transport etc. Well over half of his output was shot in Rhyl and nearly all the remainder at other Welsh locations. Twelve survive, at least in part. A thirteenth (about a dispute with the local council) survived as discontinuous fragments and has been converted into a representative series of 35mm transparencies. One other can be attributed to him on grounds of provenance. Also surviving are two films in which he appears: of a family wedding in Rhyl and of an Aberystwyth event of the 1920s.

On 28 December 1895 Lyons photographic factory owner Antoine Lumière and sons Auguste and Louis booked the *Salon Indien* in the basement of the *Grande Café*, Paris and used their *Cinematographe* invention to screen films they had shot earlier that year. The Lumières are acknowledged as the first to exhibit to the public what was soon to become a global medium of entertainment. By early 1896 their films had reached the UK and other European countries. Berry notes that they were being screened for the first time in Wales in May, as a principal item on the bill of a Cardiff music-hall. Swansea and Newport followed in July.

In December 1896, a mere 12 months after the Lumières' pioneering event, Arthur Cheetham undertook a short tour to exhibit films in three towns near Rhyl. In January 1898 he became a film **maker**. Until 1906, when he opened his first permanent cinema, he would entertain Rhyl audiences at various times of the year, particularly during Whit-week. His favourite venue was the Town Hall, which he would book for one, three or even six evenings, and where his grandson Stanley Cheetham unveiled a plaque in his honour in 1997 during the film centenary celebrations. After the holiday season he would tour, screening films at towns in England as well as in Wales.

The international nature of the infant film industry is exemplified by Cheetham's screening of the work of early producers such as Georges Méliès of France, the Edison Manufacturing Company of the USA, south Wales fairground showman William Haggar, Blackburn's Mitchell & Kenyon and several operating in London and the Brighton area. Films lasted typically for about a minute when Cheetham started, although some of his early productions were rather longer. But well before he opened his first cinema, dramatic films in particular could last for at least 10 minutes.

Identifying films acquired by Cheetham has often proved difficult. Titles did not appear on early ones, and if an exhibitor didn't fancy the title given by a producer he might change it. Some topics would become so popular that several versions with similar or varying titles were produced, while plagiaristic re-workings of popular ones can make it difficult to distinguish them from originals.

Cheetham would offer his audiences a wide range of film *genres*: 'actuality' (simple scenes from everyday life), 'interest' (the embryonic documentary, with the emphasis on the subject matter), 'topical' (portraying newsworthy events, whether genuine or re-enacted), travelogues, music-hall 'turns', drama and comedy (the last two sometimes enhanced by trick-photography).[1] With the exception of one comedy, his own output was a mixture of actualities, interest films and topicals in roughly equal proportions. Shot with a stationary camera and comprising single scenes, his early efforts are seen by Berry as 'nestling comfortably in the mainstream of early British shorts, providing insights into the popular subject matter and technical shortcomings of the day'.

Rhyl's pioneer film-maker was acutely aware of the value of publicity, and much can be gleaned about him from the previews, advertisements and reports on his shows in the *Rhyl Journal* and the *Rhyl Record and Advertiser*. Although both papers give some indication of the films screened, their coverage was not always comprehensive. Those listed in his advertisements were frequently followed tantalisingly by '&c., &c.' or 'See bills and circulars'. He would also play gramophone

---

[1] Review of *genres* based on the classification in Rachael Low and Roger Manvell's *The History of the British Film, volume 1: 1896–1906*, pp. 51-110

records for his audiences and offer them live entertainment in the form of songs (often illustrated by magic-lantern slides), instrumental solos and duets, sketches, ventriloquism etc.

Some film exhibitors visiting Rhyl would hire venues for lengthy periods in the holiday season. For example, Edison's Animated Pictures ('direct from St James' Great Hall, Manchester') occupied the Bijou Pavilion on the pier for eleven weeks in 1901. 'If people got it into their heads that he was *the* Edison', wrote early English film-maker Cecil Hepworth about the company's colourful principal in his autobiography *Came the Dawn*, 'that was their look-out'. *The* Edison was, of course, Thomas Alva Edison, proprietor of the Edison Manufacturing Company. Edison's Animated Pictures returned to the Bijou for five weeks in 1903, when they screened two Méliès films. In the 10-minute *Barbe Bleu / Blue Beard*, the eponymous villain's young bride is rescued by her sister, her seven brothers and a good fairy. The 14-minute sci-fi *Le Voyage dans la Lune / A Trip to the Moon* tells the tale of a rocket-full of intrepid space-travellers who escape the clutches of the fierce Lunars before returning to Earth. Films produced by Méliès employed a wide range of trick-photography, as shown in the on-line Internet Archive's *Georges Méliès Collection*.

Also visiting Rhyl were New Century Pictures of Leeds, who opened at the Bijou on Whit Monday 1905 and stayed for over 18 weeks. One of the films they screened was Hepworth's six-minute drama *Rescued by Rover*. Its canine hero leads a distraught father to his abducted infant daughter.[2] Two of the

---

[2] Cecil Hepworth had spent some time in London with Maguire & Baucus (Edison's European agents) and their film-producing successors the Warwick Trading Company before setting up his own production company. *Rescued by Rover* was among the films produced at his Walton-on-Thames studio (Luke McKernan in the on-line *Who's Who of Victorian Cinema*)

films screened by New Century during their return to Rhyl in 1906 were by Edison. The unemployed hero of *The Ex-convict* turns burglar for his sick daughter's sake. But he is forgiven, having previously saved the life of his wealthy victim's child. In *The Kleptomaniac* a wealthy compulsive thief steals from a departmental store. She is freed by the court. But a poor woman who takes a much-needed loaf from an unattended basket is imprisoned.

The Edison, Méliès and Hepworth films described above can be viewed on *YouTube*. So can others of UK, French and US origin to be mentioned later in this book. Some Cheetham films can be viewed on-line on the British Film Institute's *'Britain on Film' BFI Player* by googling the title on a compatible browser and selecting the appropriate entry. Their *Screenonline: 1890s Films* and *Screenonline: 1900s Films* are also relevant. Both can be consulted initially for titles, synopses and background information before viewing individual films at any registered UK school, college, university or public library.

Chapter 1

Resourceful Businessman

Arthur Cheetham was born in rural Derbyshire in 1865, the son of a farm labourer. When I interviewed his daughter Mrs Gwen Cordery at her Cheadle home in 1977, she told me that he had been apprenticed to a Derby printer before moving to Manchester, where he worked for a phrenologist in the Barton Arcade. When he and his wife arrived at Rhyl in the summer of 1889 they set up home in Sussex Street, near the beach. The *Rhyl Record and Advertiser*'s 'Fashionable List of Visitors, Householders, Public Buildings, Places of Worship, &c.' described him as a 'Mental Scientist and Medical Electrician'.

Advertisements placed in the *Rhyl Journal* for Whit Saturday, 24 May 1890 by several entertainment venues signalled the start of that year's holiday season. The next issue reported that Cheetham had begun his twice-daily foreshore lectures, speaking to 'large and appreciative audiences every morning and evening on Phrenology, Health, &c.', that 'the public delineations of character have shown that Mr Cheetham is a most clever exponent of the science' and that 'the lectures will now be continuing during the season'. He was already giving private character delineations, advice on health and treatment with his electro-curative battery at his premises. The battery, he claimed in his weekly *Record and Advertiser* advertisement, was useful for indigestion, nervousness, sciatica, shock to the system, rheumatism, paralysis, weak eyes, lumbago, strokes, constipation, throat weakness, pleurisy, gout, toothache, neuralgia, headache etc. It had been designed for home use, and various sizes were available for inspection, together with testimonials from satisfied clients.

In 1983, I recorded two elderly Rhyl residents' recollections of Cheetham: Mr Albert Edwards, retired Clerk of Rhyl Urban District Council, and 97-year-old Mrs Adelaide Clarke. Mr Edwards and his brother had lived in a house on the Promenade as boys, spending their summer holidays on the sands. 'I have vivid memories of Cheetham's phrenology stand', he said. 'I didn't know the word "Phrenology". We used to call it "reading the bumps". He used to invite people up on the platform and read their bumps. And particularly, I think, he used to get children [to go up] because the parents wanted to know what careers or schools they could set them to.' Mrs Clarke observed: 'Parents realized that Mr Cheetham had a gift and they used to take their children [to him]. They willingly paid a shilling for reading the bumps ... I listened to his phrenology talks but I never gave him a shilling for telling me my bumps. I had more dignity [knowing chortle]'.

After reminiscing at length on her father's varied career during her 1977 interview, Mrs Cordery gave me a card-mounted photograph of his foreshore stand, festooned with posters for his battery and his lectures on 'Heads', 'Faces', 'Bumps' and 'The Use of Phrenology'. 'Why are the audience facing the wrong way?' I asked. 'The people used to turn round', she explained, 'and he used to take a picture of them, and all the children sitting on the beach in front and the adults behind.' On the back of the card were instructions for purchasing copies (extra ones by sending the reference number and postage stamps to 'A. Cheetham, Stationer, Rhyl'). As to the private character delineations, Mrs Cordery explained: 'He used to work ... at home with these consultations, dictate them into a phonograph, and then Mother used to type them out onto sheets for the people. He could tell by looking at you what your character was without feeling your head ... Suppose a lady wanted to find the right man for herself. She used to send him a photograph and ask him to look at it and read his character for her. If he was the wrong man, she would let him go'.

Cheetham was advertising himself in the local papers as 'Professor of Mental Science and Electrician' in 1890. But by 1891, having moved to adjacent Queen Street, he had become a 'Registered Professional Phrenologist (Member of the British Phrenological Association.) and Medical Electrician'. His new premises boasted 'Special Rooms for consultations and Electric Treatment, and a Spacious Waiting Room'. Bath treatment followed in 1892, with Mrs Cheetham catering for the ladies. The *Record and Advertiser* was full of admiration for his foreshore appearances during the 1893 Whit-week: '[he] descanted from an elegant, enclosed rostrum [and] attracted considerable congregations ... his versatility of resource enables him both to amuse and edify his hearers, whilst his public delineations of character lend added interest to his lectures'. In August he 'drew large concourses of people around his rostrum [and] treated his subjects with all the lucidity they demanded, and varied them with the most pleasing humour'.

Newspaper reports for Whit and August Bank Holiday weeks continued to mention Cheetham's foreshore appearances, usually in sympathetic terms. For example, reporting on Whit-week 1896, the *Journal* remonstrated: 'it is not fair to Mr Tom Wood [a concert-party proprietor] and Mr Cheetham, who pay very large sums for the privilege of giving entertainments on the front, to have them disturbed by ugly-mugged and long-lung Salvationists, who pay nothing, but collar all they can get'. And in August 1904, while acknowledging that the 'Merrie Men' concert-party drew 'vast crowds of people who appeared to greatly enjoy their songs, their jokes, their quips and cranks and mirth-provoking sketches', the *Record and Advertiser* noted: 'Professor Cheetham entertained the most intelligent section of the crowd by his lucid and bright phrenological lectures'. Conversely, it had observed sceptically in 1901: 'the attendance at Professor Cheetham's lectures proves that there are many believers in Phrenology or at all events, that the Professor possesses the ability to interest and entertain his patrons'.

Although Cheetham's foreshore appearances finished in 1904, the opening of his Rhyl cinema in 1906 did not preclude the continued use of his Queen Street premises. Advertisements in his 1908 weekly film programme-booklet offered both electric treatment for a host of ailments by 'Cheetham's 20th Century Battery' and 'your character ... scientifically described by A. Cheetham, the only local representative and member of the British Incorporated Phrenological Society'.[1]

By 1895 Arthur Cheetham had gained sufficient standing locally to participate in a traditional end-of-season event: a 'benefit' concert for a fellow-entertainer. Pier-head diver 'Professor' Frank Sinclair was to be honoured on this occasion. Among the participants were the members of two concert parties. There were also swimming races, foot races, diving competitions, Sinclair's own 'Swimming Entertainment' and high diving. December 1896 saw Cheetham's first recorded

---

[1] *Programme. SILVOGRAPH ANIMATED PICTURES. CENTRAL HALL, Market Street, RHYL.* [1908], p. 6: the Cinema Museum

involvement in civic affairs. At a meeting called by the local council to consider advertising Rhyl, he agreed that 'the Councillors should take part in the movement, as they knew how to get money, especially when they raised rents 140 per cent'. He suggested that lighting the Promenade by electricity would advertise the town, 'as the front would then be the finest in the United Kingdom'. He was duly elected to the committee set up to take the appropriate steps.

The publications Cheetham produced in 1893 and 1894 reflect his interests and presumed fields of expertise. *Curative Electricity: a Manual for the Home Treatment of Disease* (containing 'exposures of all Modern Electrical Frauds') was the first, priced at one shilling (5p in today's money, ignoring inflation of well over 100%). Then followed *The Real Truth about Electricity in Relation to Health*. His *Character Reading Practically Explained* and *Phrenology in a Nutshell* were both reprinted, while his *Noses: And how to Read Them* was based on one of his lectures. After the appearance of *Indigestion: How to Prevent and Cure it*, he entered the realms of counselling with *Tempers and how to Control Them* and *Courtship and Marriage: How to Court and When to Marry*. While *Curative Electricity* was 121 pages long, his other publications varied between eight and 20 pages. But he managed to cover the comprehensive topic of *Health and Happiness: a Compendium of Useful Information* in all of ten pages![2]

One of his customers was Cecil Hepworth, whose 1903 catalogue he printed.[3] His publication *The Rhyl Pilot* advised readers 'where to go, what to see, and what to do' in and around the town.[4] And the form he completed in 1899 to apply to the local council for permission to convert a cottage at the rear of

[2] Cheetham's publications: researched by Charles Evans-Günther
[3] Hepworth catalogue: the Cinema Museum
[4] *The Rhyl Pilot*: Flintshire Record Office (ref D/DM/919.44)

his premises into a workroom had been printed by none other than 'Arthur Cheetham, Printer, 30, Queen Street, Rhyl'![5]

Several of his photographs graced the pages of J.D. Polkinghorne's *Bracing Rhyl* of 1900. One of them is an evocative view of the beach, with the pier as a back-drop. His full-page advertisement in this publication draws attention to his 'Views of Rhyl'. Readers are invited to examine them in his window and 'notice the difference in sharpness and clearness between these **Genuine Photographs** and the printed collotype imitations usually sold'. The films he had been shooting since January 1898 are not mentioned.

Arthur Cheetham claims to have pioneered the use of electric light in Rhyl, both at his Queen Street premises and with an arc lamp outside in time for the town's 1894 May Day parade (an annual event established in 1891 to celebrate the start of the holiday season). But it was March 1901 before any other businesses in town enjoyed this facility, introduced not by Cheetham but by local company Messrs D.P. Jones. Reporting on the work done by them for a High Street chemist, the *Journal* understood that there was 'a large number of contracts in hand' and commended the chemist for having the wiring done 'before the busy time sets in'.

Arthur Cheetham was not without his detractors. The *Record and Advertiser* report on the local council's May 1901 meeting mentions a petition from residents of West Parade (part of the Promenade) concerning his foreshore stand. One councillor talked of complaints about 'the same nuisance season after season'. Another one suggested he be removed to the island in the middle of the Marine Lake (at the western end of town, some distance from the Promenade) 'where he would be far

---

[5] Application form: Flintshire Record Office (ref Rhyl UDC)

enough away from everybody'. But others supported him, and the council eventually referred the matter to a committee in the hope of finding a site 'which would be less objectionable, and at the same time satisfactory to Mr. Cheetham'.

However, Rhyl's intrepid entertainer was not to be outdone. Nearing the end of his annual tour, he reacted promptly from Welshpool, mid-Wales with a letter to the editor. The matter under discussion was, he explained, that of two young men who had played a gramophone at his stand during the previous year – with the council's permission. This should have been mentioned at the meeting, although he had decided not to allow any such arrangements in future. It would have been more charitable of the petitioners to speak to him personally and try to arrange matters in a kindly manner. He had never had a single complaint during the twelve years he had spoken on the shore. 'It is a strange thing', he notes, 'that this petition should have been rushed on the Council while it is a well-known fact that I am away from home and therefore unable to speak for myself'. It appears, however, that the council took no further action. The matter was not raised in the June or July meetings, and the well-established foreshore appearances continued.

In 1912, when he was a member of the local council, Arthur Cheetham paraded his assumed scientific expertise as chairman of a Town Hall meeting held by the non-militant National Union of Women's Suffrage Societies. Although he had been elected as 'a business candidate, independent of politics, party or creed', he was clearly not without convictions. The audience applauded when he declared that he had advocated the equality of men and women ever since becoming a public man. He then explained that, although the male brain was a little larger on average than the female one, the latter was much finer, with the advantage of greater intuitive power. More applause. 'The voting power of women', he concluded, 'is much wanted to set right many things affecting humanity, morality, and the advantage of the welfare of the world at large'. Final applause. A motion calling on Parliament to pass some measure of women's suffrage that year was unanimously adopted. But six years were to elapse before certain categories of women gained the vote, and the equality advocated by Cheetham was not achieved until 1928.

Chapter 2

August 1896: 'the latest and greatest London sensation'

1896 was the year when films were first screened to audiences in Rhyl – not through the efforts of Arthur Cheetham, but during the three-day visit of a touring concert-party to one of the town's theatres at the height of the holiday season. At that time Summer Bank Holiday in England and Wales fell on the first Monday in August. The *Rhyl Journal* reported on the influx of visitors: 'Fortunately the weather on Saturday was beautifully fine, and a visit to the railway station about the middle of the afternoon made clear that Rhyl would have a busy Bank Holiday ... every down train [i.e. 'down' from Euston] which arrived appeared to almost empty itself at this place ... Where the crowds of visitors who continued to arrive until a late hour found accommodation is a mystery ... The streets were crowded until a late hour, and on Sunday the Promenade was literally packed from one end to the other'. Monday was also fine, and 'at the railway station about 14,000 persons were dealt with'.

The pier hosted several attractions. 'Professor' Frank Sinclair and members of the local swimming club gave demonstrations of diving and swimming, and a Mr MacCann won the prize for 'walking the greasy bowsprit'. The Grand Pavilion at the pier entrance staged afternoon shows by Jimmy Charters's 'Nigger Troupe' (who would 'black-up') and evening concerts by Mr Vetter's resident orchestra.

One of the small refreshment rooms on the pier housed

'some of Edison's novelties'. These seem to have been Kinetoscopes, the coin-operated viewers developed by Edison's employee W.K. Dickson. Patrons would view moving images on endless loops of film transported through the machine's mechanism at a speed of about 40 frames per second – as opposed to the then usual 16-or-so for films viewed on screen. They would last for less than a minute and feature such topics as a barber-shop, a bar-room, a female dancer in a voluminous dress and a cock-fight. The words 'some of ...' suggest an arrangement similar to the 'kinetoscope parlors' which originated in the USA. A contemporary drawing of the first 'parlor', at 1155 Broadway, New York City, reproduced by courtesy of Professor Charles Musser of Yale University, appears on page ii.

The Langford and Christie's 'At Homes' company at the Bijou Pavilion (then called the Small Pavilion on the Pier) were in their third season at Rhyl, presenting 'Recitals, Music, Songs, Dramatic Sketches, Humorous and Musical Sketches, Living Pictures'. Although 'living pictures' was an early term for ciné film, those presented at the Small Pavilion were merely 'Mr Langford's inimitable facial entertainment'.

Jimmy Charters had been a member of Tom Wood's concert-party. But, as the *Journal* had reported earlier in the year: 'there has unfortunately been a split in the nigger troupe performing on the sands ... in order to provide proper accommodation [on the pier] several structural alterations will be made at that place'. Result: more choice for visitors, since Wood continued to occupy the pitch on the sands.

Messrs Gilding and Jones's band gave promenade concerts each evening featuring current soloist Mme Emilie Young, as well as performing at various locations around the town during the day.

Touring companies offered a choice of comedy and drama at two venues in town that week. Fred Smith's Comedy and Burlesque Company staged a 'Highly Comic Operatic Burlesque in two Acts' called *Robinson Crusoe* at the Town Hall on Monday, Tuesday and Wednesday. Then, on Thursday, Friday and Saturday his No. 1 'Trilby Co' played 'the Great Play – TRILBY In Four Acts'.

Ten years later the Operetta House, a music-hall above a row of shops in town-centre Market Street, would become Arthur Cheetham's first permanent cinema. But during August Bank Holiday week 1896 three evenings of 'the Screaming Farcical Comedy – "The New Baby" ' played by Mr Arthur Bourchier's No. 1 Company ('from the Royalty Theatre, London') were followed by three of W.E. Langley's Company with 'the powerful drama in four Acts, entitled "The Scarlet Brotherhood".

The Palace Theatre, at the west end of Rhyl, stood next to the 35-acre Summer Gardens, with their seal pond, aviary, monkey-house, cycle-track, tennis courts, cricket and football pitches, bandstand and switchback railway. The 1898 film *A Switchback Railway*, produced by English film-maker R.W. Paul, shows this type of attraction in action.[1] A night-time activity was skating through avenues illuminated by fairy-lights. That week, Palace Theatre proprietor Edward Neville's resident repertory company performed four different shows: *My Sweetheart* on Monday and Tuesday, *Trilby* on Wednesday,

---

[1] R.W. Paul had been an electrical instrument maker in London. His career in film, lasting until 1910, included the production of comic and dramatic films at his studio and processing laboratory in Muswell Hill, London (John Barnes in *Who's Who of Victorian Cinema*)

The New Private Secretary on Thursday and Friday, and *The New Magdalen* on Saturday.

Bank-holiday week ended with a lifeboat-day on Saturday, starting with swimming races at the pier-head by members of the lifeboat crew ('in full Lifeboat Costume') and a life-saving demonstration. The afternoon's 'Grand Procession of Lifeboat and Ladies' Crews' was followed by rowing and swimming races and 'a Burlesque Aquatic Sketch' by the Swimming Club at the Marine Lake. At 8.30 pm the lifeboat took part in a second procession. Finally, at 10 o'clock, it was launched from the beach and followed to the pier-head by illuminated boats.

On the following Monday, Tuesday and Wednesday the Palace Theatre welcomed a return visit of the '50 talented artistes' of the Moore & Burgess Minstrels, who had started their provincial tour at Hastings during the previous week. Their regular fare of music, humour and sketches was augmented by 'the latest and greatest London sensation, ANIMATED PHOTOGRAPHS'. The *Record and Advertiser* was impressed by two of them: 'a representation of an animated scene on a Parisian Boulevard' and 'the scene in a dentist's operating room representing a group of several figures … applying gas, and extracting the tooth and of carrying out the other operations incidental to this painful process'.

The local papers give no indication of the origins of these two contrasting films. The Lumières were certainly shooting Parisian street-scenes in 1896. However, not only were their films then unavailable to independent exhibitors, but they were transported through the projector by mechanical claws engaging in circular perforations, rather than the rectangular ones used by Edison since Kinetoscope days and later adopted by other producers. In his *The A.B.C. of the Cinematograph* (1897) Cecil Hepworth explains that circular perforations 'could only be used for very short films', since 'the inertia of a larger roll could not be overcome quickly enough by the claws without tearing and destroying the film'. A drawing from a catalogue of Lumière films comparing both systems, reproduced by courtesy of James Offer, appears on page ii.

Whose film, then, was that of the 'animated scene on a Parisian Boulevard'? The Moore & Burgess Minstrels were based at St. James's Hall in London's Piccadilly. Magician David Devant was a member of a conjuring company appearing at the nearly Egyptian Hall. He introduced films produced by R. W. Paul and Georges Méliès to his audiences in 1896. Méliès was then an illusionist appearing at *Théâtre Robert-Houdin* in Paris. After his request to buy a *Cinematographe* from the Lumières was refused, he obtained a projector of Paul's making to screen films by Paul and Edison. He then converted it into a camera and started filming in May. The titles of films advertised by Devant in August correspond to some of those produced by Méliès – Paris street-scenes being among them. So Moore & Burgess could have acquired one of them from Devant in time for their visit to Rhyl.[2]

If the 'scene in a dentist's operating room' was Edison's *In The Dentist's Chair* (featuring a Dr Coulton, reputedly the first to use gas for extracting teeth) it could have been supplied by the film-maker's agents, Maguire and Baucus. So a *Rhyl Journal* reference to 'the marvelous Edison invention' presented by the Minstrels may not have been entirely without basis.

---

[2] Devant, Moore & Burgess and Méliès: John Barnes on Devant and David Robinson on Méliès in *Who's Who of Victorian Cinema* and Barnes on Moore & Burgess in his *The Beginnings of the Cinema in England: Volume 1 1894–1896*, pp. 201, 203

Of course, Arthur Cheetham was likely to have been as busy on those three days as he had been the week before, when (as the *Record and Advertiser* explained) he had 'the opportunity of uttering words of wisdom to immense audiences' at his foreshore stand. But whether or not he saw Moore & Burgess's presentation of 'the latest and greatest London sensation', he must surely have been aware of Rhyl's first experience of 'animated photography' projected on screen – and perhaps inspired by it, since his career in film started before the year was out. In the souvenir booklet he published in connection with the opening of his Colwyn Bay cinema in 1911, he notes that he bought his first 'Cinematograph' (projector) in December 1896 to give 'exhibitions' at the nearby Flintshire towns of Holywell, Buckley and Flint.[3] Sadly, no other record survives.

Films mentioned in this chapter which can be viewed on *YouTube*: a selection called *Edison Kinetoscope Films 1894–1896* and Paul's *A Switchback Railway*

---

[3] *Opening of the Colwyn Bay Cinema in connection with Arthur Cheetham's Picture Theatres*, [1911]. p. [8]: National Library of Wales

Chapter 3

1897: 'Living Pictures, or Animated Photographs, By the Cinematograph'

In whatever way Arthur Cheetham had publicised his Holywell, Buckley and Flint 'exhibitions' of December 1896, he used both early terms for ciné film when he advertised his 'New and Marvellous Entertainment of Living Pictures, or Animated Photographs, By the Cinematograph' at Rhyl Town Hall on Tuesday 19 January 1897. Rhyl Council chairman Abel Jones JP was to preside, but an apology for his absence due to ill-health was read out on the night. The 'Entertainment' was held under the patronage of the town's Cycling Club. Mr and Mrs Cheetham were members; she would take part in the first ladies' tour later in the year, with her husband as 'captain'.

Contrary to the impression given by the local newspaper advertisements, more time was devoted to magic-lantern slides than to films that evening. The first part of the programme comprised 'views' taken by Cheetham of Cycling Club members in camp, a series illustrating the hymn *The Rock of Ages* and 'some picturesque photographs taken … on a tour in Ireland [which] occupied the chief part of the evening'. The 'Living Pictures, or Animated Photographs' were shown after the interval, during which Cheetham expounded on their variation in length between 50 and 150 feet. Whether or not he actually said that more frames were taken per minute 'when the movements were very rapid, such as in dancing', that was the understanding of the patently ill-informed *Record and Advertiser* reporter, who singled out four of the films in this two-hour show for attention: one depicting storm-waves at a breakwater, a 'garden scene', 'Bicycling in the Park' and 'Stables on Fire'.

Not unexpectedly, the reporter likened the breakwater film, in which 'the interested sightseers above [moved] to and fro, rushing to escape the spray', to similar scenes in Rhyl. This description suggests that it was *Rough Sea at Dover* of 1895. Edison had omitted to patent his Kinetoscope in Europe, so R.W. Paul constructed and sold unauthorized replicas. He co-operated with American-born Birt Acres to produce *Rough Sea at Dover* and other films for use with them. The Paul/Acres collaboration was short-lived; both had gone their separate ways before 1896 was out, and Acres's brush with film would be brief.[1]

The breaking waves in *Rough Sea at Dover* must have appeared awesome to Cheetham's audience when projected at the slower 16-or-so frames-per-second. How different had the response been when Acres screened it to the Cardiff Photographic Society in 1896. Berry notes that rounds of applause were accorded to each wave as it rolled in! On the other hand, in his *Before the Nickelodeon. Edwin S. Porter and the Edison Manufacturing Company*, Charles Musser quotes from a review of the film's New York debut about a fortnight later: 'a diminutive roller ... apparently increasing in volume, and throwing up little jets of snow-white foam, rolling faster and faster ... until it bursts and flings its shredded masses far into the air'. Patrons in the front row were said to be inclined to leave their seats as it crashed on the beach and seeming about to flood the theatre.

---

[1] Birt Acres had been a photographer in north London before his co-operation with Paul (Richard Brown in *Who's Who of Victorian Cinema*). Berry notes that Acres's filming of the Prince and Princess of Wales at the Cardiff Fine Art, Industrial and Maritime Exhibition in 1896 resulted in an invitation to present the first royal command film-show. He also refers to Paul's production and screening of two Cardiff street-scenes that year – almost certainly the first in Wales

The *Record and Advertiser* reporter's opinion of the 'garden' film as 'remarkable' brings the celebrated Lumière comedy *L'Arroseur Arrosé / The Sprinkler Sprinkled* to mind. A gardener's water supply is interrupted by a boy treading on his hose; bemused gardener examines nozzle but is drenched when boy lifts foot off hose; boy is chased, caught and spanked – all in 19 seconds. The Lumières produced several versions in 1895 and 1896. However, their films would not be produced with rectangular perforations and available generally in the UK until May 1897, when their UK agents Fuerst Bros of London, among others, started to market them.[2] So any one of the 1896 re-workings by Acres, Edison or Méliès could have been screened that evening.

'Bicycling in the Park' appears to be Paul's *Hyde Park Bicycling Scene* of 1896, depicting a leisurely parade of pony-traps and cycles, with the ladies cyclists wearing skirts instead of the earlier female trouser-like attire. This film was surely included in Cheetham's programme in recognition of the Cycling Club's patronage of the evening's entertainment.

The *Record and Advertiser*'s description of 'Stables on Fire' as featuring 'smoke and the rescue of horses and carriages' reveals it to be Edison's *The Burning Stable*. His catalogue is more forthcoming: 'A burning wagon is dragged from the barn by the firemen, and four horses are rescued from the flames by the stablemen. Thick volumes of smoke pour from the doors and windows'.

Cheetham then embarked on a tour of over thirty Welsh towns. He returned to Rhyl Town Hall for one evening in March with a 'new silver screen (only just invented) which

---

[2] Fuerst Brothers had previously been UK agents for Lumière photographic film plates. Their film catalogues listed hundreds of the French company's actualities, interest films, topicals and comedies, as well as travelogues shot on all five continents (John Barnes in *Who's Who of Victorian Cinema*)

brings the pictures up with a brilliancy equal to electric light'. Although his newspaper advertisements mention 'new living pictures', none of them are named, the emphasis being on the live performers. Mrs Cheetham was due to give 'songs with [magic lantern] illustrations', but the newspaper reports do not mention her. Local soloist T. Amos Jones sang *The Village Blacksmith* and *Y Bachgen Dewr* (The Brave Boy). Another guest performer, Mme Marie Williamson, sang *The Better Land* and *Daddie* and gave selections on her American Concert Bells (of metal construction and akin to the xylophone) and the auto-harp (a form of chorded zither) among other instruments.

Cheetham's magic lantern was put to good use, not only to illustrate the songs but also to present his own photographs of a cycling tour and those of the previous October's storm in Rhyl taken by local resident C.H. Palethorpe. Mr Palethorpe appears to have been a person of means, since the *Journal*'s weekly 'List of Visitors' records him as living at the select eastern end of Rhyl's sea-front and not taking in visitors.

During the evening, Cheetham announced ('amid applause') that he was negotiating for taking over the Small Pavilion on the Pier for the summer. In the event, however, he merely hired the Grand Pavilion for the Easter weekend. The films screened on the Saturday and Monday were augmented by 'Songs with Pictorial Illustrations' sung by his wife and himself and humorous songs by 'Mr J.R. Williams, the well-known entertainer'. A sacred concert on the Sunday included songs (again by both Cheethams), 'musical selections', recitations (not humorous, of course) by Mr Williams and 'Pictorial Illustrations and Dissolving Effects with the magic lantern'. Mention of 'Dissolving Effects' indicates that Cheetham's lantern was quite sophisticated: either 'bi-unial' or 'tri-unial' (with two or three separate light-sources and lens systems respectively) capable of merging pictures gradually one into the other, such as day into night or the succession of the seasons. An advertisement for a bi-unial lantern, reproduced by courtesy of my former colleague David Jones, as appears on page iv.

One civic acquisition reported by the *Journal* in May was a steam-roller. This 'long-expected and sadly-wanted' machine had just arrived, and the work of road-making in town had begun. It was to provide Cheetham with material for filming in the following year (his first as a film **maker**). And the paper's 25 December issue serves as a reminder of his diverse commercial interests. The survey 'Around the Shops at Christmastide' reported the windows of his Queen Street premises to be 'well-filled with Christmas cards and fancy goods adaptable to all customers'.

Films mentioned in this chapter which can be viewed on *YouTube*: *Rough Sea at Dover*, (Paul/Acres), *L'Arroseur Arrosé / The Sprinkler Sprinkled* (Lumière), the surviving 20 seconds of *Hyde Park Bicycling Scene* (Paul) and *The Burning Stable* (Edison)

Chapter 4

1898: 'Local Living Pictures'

1898 was to be Arthur Cheetham's first year as a film-maker. But those he screened on a January evening at Rhyl Town Hall during a break in his winter tour were all by other pioneers. While the *Journal's* preview merely refers to 'another grand entertainment', the *Record and Advertiser* drew readers' attention to films about an incident in the brief Græco-Turkish war of 1897 and Queen Victoria's diamond jubilee celebrations.

This was the first time that Cheetham called his show 'Silvograph'. He would continue to do so well into his cinema-owning days. That was not the only innovation offered for that evening. The *Journal* loyally announced that 'his pictures ... are now 12 ft wide, and shown with a jet capable of giving 2,000 candle light' – confirmation that his film projector (like his magic lantern) was still illuminated by 'limelight', produced by heating a cylinder of quicklime (calcium oxide) to a very high temperature with an oxy-hydrogen flame emanating from a tube called a 'jet'. A diagram of a jet, reproduced by courtesy of my former colleague David Jones, appears on page iv.

The war between Greece and Turkey had been fought over the status of Crete. The island was a Turkish province, although the Greek majority favoured *Enosis* (union with their homeland). After the armistice, it became an autonomous state with Greek Prince George as High Commissioner. The film described by the *Record and Advertiser* as depicting 'the man of war "George" shelling Previsu' was *Combat Naval en Grèce / Naval Combat in Greece*, one of four Méliès *actualités reconstituées* (re-enactments) about the war: an officer orders sailors to man a cannon, but after two hits from Turkish artillery the smoke clears to reveal one sailor lying prostrate. The action on the swaying deck, complete with actors, theatrical 'props' and painted scenery, had been filmed in a Paris garden by a camera trained on a set which swayed from side to side.

A football film screened that evening can't have featured major teams, since the *Record and Advertiser* observed: 'the cries of "goal" when the ball was shown flying through [sic] the posts reminded one of £1000 "gates" at a league match'. R.W. Paul had shot a football film at Newcastle-on-Tyne in 1896, but his catalogue gives no indication of the status of the game. Three others date from 1897: by opticians/camera-makers Watson & Sons of Holborn, G.A. Smith at his St Anne's Well pleasure garden in Hove[1] and Spanish producer Alexandre Promio for the Lumières. No details of the Watson film are available; and no goal is scored from the corner-kick captured by Smith during a gardeners' game or in Promio's *Football*, featuring a crowded goalmouth on a practice pitch. So the film which inspired the cries of 'goal' must remain unidentified.

For the *Record and Advertiser*, the evening's 'crisis of excitement' was reached by the screening of a film portraying 'the Queen's Carriage and Life Guards following'. Up to 20 producers are known to have mounted their cameras along the seven-mile route from Buckingham Palace to St. Paul's Cathedral and back for the Diamond Jubilee procession of 22 June 1897. Footage of the Queen in her carriage had already been screened at a private Balmoral film-show, so there might have been some justification for Cheetham's boastful

---

[1] Apart from being the location of his 1897 football film, G.A. Smith's St Anne's Well pleasure garden housed both a film studio and equipment for processing his own productions and those of contemporaries (Frank Gray in *Who's Who of Victorian Cinema*)

newspaper advertisements claiming 'as shown at Balmoral before Her Majesty the Queen' (albeit not by him!). The record for getting coverage of the celebrations to market must belong to R.J. Appleton & Co, whose film had been processed on a train bound for their native Bradford the same day. Thousands of their fellow townsfolk turned out to view it in the open air at midnight.[2] Rhyl had to wait for over six months!

One choice piece of information appears to have been entrusted exclusively to the *Record and Advertiser*. Its preview of the show had referred enigmatically to 'a startling surprise which we are not permitted to divulge'. All became clear on the night, when Cheetham threw on the screen a film of Rhyl beach 'which he had personally taken only the preceding Friday'. 'This picture', observed the newspaper's report condescendingly, 'was (considering it was a first attempt) a grand success, and the children on the picture were at once recognised by the audience.' In the booklet published for the opening of his Colwyn Bay cinema in 1911, Cheetham explains how his 'machine for taking animated photographs' had been constructed 'by an ingenious adaptation of the mechanical part of the Cinematograph he was using for the projection of the Pictures'. After developing the film, he converted his 'machine' into a printer to produce a positive 'show' copy from the original negative. However ingenious, he was by no means first in the field. A re-arrangement of components had enabled the Lumières' *Cinématographe* to function as camera, printer and projector.

The *Record and Advertiser*'s report is the first reference to Cheetham's use of a pianist to accompany films. Needless to say, he or she (un-named) also played for Mrs Cheetham when

---

[2] R. J. Appleton & Co had been photographic and magic-lantern suppliers for about 20 years before the advent of film. Their open-air Diamond Jubilee film-show was repeated nightly for a week and is reputed to have attracted over 250,000 spectators (Richard Brown and Denis Gifford in *Who's Who of Victorian Cinema*)

she sang *The Holy City* and *The Toilers,* (both illustrated with 'magnificent colour slides'). Slides also depicted Cycling Club activities, north Wales views and a North Wales Coast League football match played on Boxing Day between Rhyl Town and Rhyl Amateurs. Town had won 5-1, thus staying top of the table, ahead of Llandudno, Bangor, the Amateurs, Holywell and Caernarfon. But the paper commented diplomatically: 'Unfortunately, the visitors were without their goalkeeper, and this in some measure accounts for the somewhat heavy score recorded against them'.

During his January show Cheetham had announced his intention of taking 'other animated pictures of local interest and [giving] another entertainment at an early date'. He realised his aim (and more) in late March, when he screened 13 new films at the Grand Pavilion on the pier. Footage shot at Rhyl railway station featured the Irish Mail passing through at speed, the District Inspector's single-carriage train and the arrival of a stopping train. The results of a tour in mid and north Wales were *Ladies Boating in Aberystwyth Bay*; *Loading Slates in the Docks at Portmadoc*; *A Diver at Work in Holyhead Docks*; *Arrival of the Irish Mail Boat at Holyhead*; *An Express Train Catching Mail Bags*; *Arrival of a Train at Llanrwst*; *Horse Fair at Llangollen* and *Street Scene in High Street, Wrexham.* Two other local films featured another Town v Amateurs football game and a rough sea at Rhyl.

Both local papers reported on the evening's entertainment at length. The *Journal* was most impressed by 'the animated picture of the rough sea ... which had been specially prepared for the entertainment and arrived by train from London [where it had been processed] that night'. 'The scene being a familiar one', observed the *Record and Advertiser,* 'it afforded an opportunity to those present of realising the absolute faithfulness with which the cinematograph is capable of reproducing the movements of life in man and nature.' It deemed the Holyhead mailboat film 'particularly distinct and clear', adding that 'all the movements of the boat as she made for the [landing] stage to the lowering of the gangway were reproduced with the clearest fidelity to the minutest detail'. Today's viewers can judge this assessment for themselves, since this is the only one of Cheetham's early 1898 efforts to survive. Its Rhyl screening was not, however, the first. It had been seen three times at Holyhead about a fortnight earlier under the patronage of none other than the mailboat captain.

The football fans present were, reported the *Record and Advertiser*, moved to 'exuberant enthusiasm' by the Town v Amateurs film – result: 1-1. Incidentally, the Town team ended the season second in the table to Bangor, with the Amateurs far behind. Also screened was a film by Birt Acres of the inaugural Sheriff's Shield football match, played eight days earlier at London's Crystal Palace and intended to be an annual event between English amateur and professional teams in aid of hospitals and other charities. It must have been a draw, since the six-foot trophy was shared by the Corinthian amateurs and the professional Sheffield United. The *Record and Advertiser* reporter can't have been familiar with their strips, enthusing as he did on 'the manner in which the goalkeeper of one of the teams fisted out a deadly shot upon his charge'. However, an advertisement in the theatrical weekly *The Era* identifies him as a Corinthian.

Cheetham's magic lantern was also in action that evening, showing North Wales views, 'effects' slides, the illustrations for Mrs Cheetham's rendition of *Anchored* and *The Toilers* and 'photographs of a number of Rhyl's public men, who have lent their patronage to the entertainment'. They included the chairman, vice-chairman and members of the local council, JPs and county councillors. All sixteen were solicitously listed at the head of the *Record and Advertiser* advertisement.

An advertisement in the *Record and Advertiser* in May announced Cheetham's intention of showing 'local animated photographs of Rhyl and neighbourhood' at the Town Hall about once a month, augmented by 'the Latest American Loud-speaking Talking Machine, The Gramophone'. The series started on Whit Monday and Tuesday and included two new films taken by him in town-centre Queen Street. They featured the annual May Day procession and various local characters respectively. The 'Loud-speaking Talking Machine' played orchestral selections, banjo duets, vocal quartets etc. Whit-week Silvograph shows were to become a regular feature of the Rhyl holiday scene.

Pride of place in Rhyl May Day processions was accorded to the reigning 'Queen' and her retinue. Apart from numerous tradesmen's entries, the 1898 turnout included brass bands, the local fire brigade, the new lifeboat, cyclists in fancy dress and councillors riding in landaus. But for the *Journal*, the 'great feature of the day' was the horse-drawn 'lurry' (lorry) carrying the Rhyl Royal Victoria Free Cot tableau. The cot was available to poor children at the local children's hospital / convalescent home, financed by a fund commemorating the town's 1897 jubilee celebrations. Seven-year-old Frances Cheetham was a 'nurse' in the tableau, while her brothers, eight-year-old Gustavus and five-year-old Bernard, were in another one entitled 'Rhyl Sands'. When the procession reached Queen Street, their father was waiting, camera at the ready. Were his children granted more than their fair share of footage? We will never know, since the film hasn't survived.

Both local papers had been invited to a private viewing of the May Day film and the one featuring local characters at Cheetham's Queen Street premises. The *Record and Advertiser* provides a vivid description of the latter. It waxes eloquently on 'the cumbrous movements' of the steam-roller and 'the multitude of other incidents … including a bicycle collision, the upsetting of a pot-cart, of a milk-pail, of a bucket of water &c'. One wonders whether some of the 'other incidents' in this 'most amusing' film had been choreographed by the film-maker. A reference to 'a startling novelty' must have made readers inquisitive. But all became clear when the films received their Whit Monday Town Hall screening. 'Much laughter was evoked by the procession being shown … as moving backwards by means of the latest invention in connection with the cinematograph', reported the *Record and Advertiser*. How precisely was this accomplished? 'By an arrangement of glasses', explained the *Journal* knowingly, not realising that the film had simply been run through the projector in reverse!

Cheetham kept his 'about once a month' promise, although his next efforts were not strictly local. In July and August he screened films he had taken of a concert-party on Colwyn Bay beach, a train arriving and departing at Penmaen-mawr station and the crowd leaving Llandudno's 'Happy Valley' (presumably after a show at its open-air theatre). In late August he attempted to add to his repertoire. The *Record and Advertiser* dated Saturday the 27th but on sale on the Friday (as was the custom) invited Rhyl Swimming Club members to the Marine Lake on the following afternoon to be filmed 'diving, &c. (weather permitting)' by him. There is no record of a film being shot, so perhaps the weather or the turnout or both proved to be disappointing.

In late September the *Journal* reported that Cheetham had constructed a camera capable of taking 1,000 feet of film, which he intended using for the first time at the forthcoming Blackburn Rovers v West Bromwich Albion football match, 'for which he has special permission of the club'. 'If this picture turns out well', the paper hoped, 'Mr Cheetham may let the Rhyl people have an opportunity of seeing it before he starts touring for the winter.' He gave them the opportunity within days. According to the periodical *Photography*, the resultant film lasted for just over four minutes. About 40 seconds have survived. Taken from behind one of the goals at Blackburn's Ewood Park, this fragment is devoted mainly to the first half of the game. Much of the action takes place towards the far end of the field, and the West Bromwich goalkeeper is seen pacing to and fro between the posts. The second half is featured in the last few seconds, but this short section is marred by progressive disintegration.

Wherever else Cheetham took his Silvograph show on tour, it ran at Blackburn's Exchange Hall for five nights in October. His wife had adopted her maiden name for public performances by then, appearing as 'Madame Rose Garton, Mezzo-Soprano'. Apart from her illustrated songs and the gramophone selections, the 'Grand Variety Entertainment' advertised in the *Northern Daily Telegraph* included character comedian Vert Vardo and champion clog, top-boot and sand dancer Will Mack. As to the football film: the next issue noted that 'the photographer has endeavoured to get in some of the most exciting incidents of the game, one of the goals scored by the Rovers being conspicuous from the rest'. But 'one wonders if the film records the punch that Reader [the West Bromwich goalkeeper] landed on Jackson (after he had been brought to the ground by him) whilst everyone was watching the ball in the Rovers' goal?' *Plus ça change* ... ! Never mind, the Rovers won 4-1 in front of about 5,000 spectators, and their victory took them to the top of the Football League table. To no avail, however, since they ended the season in sixth position, behind Aston Villa, Liverpool, Burnley, Everton and Notts County.[3]

In his first year as a film-maker, Arthur Cheetham had trained his camera on 20 scenes or events. His May Day effort was reported by the *Record and Advertiser* as being twice the length of his earlier ones. Assuming the surviving Holyhead mailboat film to be typical, it appears that his 1898 output lasted for little more than half an hour. Hence the value of his wife's contribution and those of other performers, the magic lantern, gramophone records and commercially-available films to his provision of about two hours' entertainment in those early days of cinema.

Films mentioned in this chapter which can be viewed on *YouTube*: *Combat Naval en Grèce* / *Naval Combat in Greece* (Méliès), *Football (1897)*, *London* (Promio) and various compilations of Queen Victoria's Diamond Jubilee procession

Combat Naval en Grèce / *Naval Combat in Greece* can also be seen on-line on *Internet Archive – The Georges Méliès Collection*. One viewer's comment: 'what struck me was how the boat rocked. Heck, if it was in a hurricane it never would have rocked THIS fast!'

---

[3] The *Northern Daily Telegraph* advertisement and report, confirmation of the venue and identification of the Rovers by their strip were provided by Robin Whalley of Blackburn

On the *Mail Online Sport* website (together with five 'stills'): *Blackburn Rovers v West Bromwich Albion, 1898* (Cheetham)

On *BFI Screenonline 1890s films*: *Holyhead Mail Boat* (Cheetham)

Chapter 5

1899: Royalty and Seaside Fun

A royal tour and the attractions of Rhyl beach were to make 1899 Arthur Cheetham's second year as a film-maker. But first of all, on one evening in January after 'a successful tour in over 20 English towns' he obliged his fellow townsfolk with a repeat screening of his Blackburn football film. Top of the bill, however, in his newspaper advertisements was Paul's *Sirdar's Reception at Guildhall*. Dating from the previous November, this film provided fleeting glimpses of Lord Kitchener's arrival in an open carriage to receive the freedom of the City of London. It was advertised by Cheetham as 'Lord Kitchener at the Guildhall', perhaps in case his audience were not familiar with the celebrated soldier's title as C-in-C of the Anglo-Egyptian Army in the Sudan earlier in the decade.

One of the three comic films advertised was 'Making Sausages'. In the American Mutoscope & Biograph Company's *The Sausage Factory* of 1897 small dogs and cats are dropped into a hopper as ingredients and leave unseen to be 'used' over and over again. The machine is prominently labelled 'Catchem' and 'Stuffem'. Cheetham could not have shown this film, since Mutoscope & Biograph films were 70mm wide at that time and exhibited at selected venues only.[1] But G.A. Smith's *Making Sausages* of 1897, in which cats and dogs are

---

[1] The American Mutoscope & Biograph Company's UK operation started screening films among the 'turns' at London's Palace Theatre of Varieties in March 1897. Their superior quality stemmed from their width, the size of the picture on the screen, the speed of projection (about 40 fps) and the efficiency of the projector's light-source (John Barnes. *The Beginnings of the Cinema in England 1894–1901, Volume Two: 1897*, pp. 143-147, 149)

complemented by a duck and an old boot 'to give flavour', would be available.

The title 'Pillow Fight' suggests a boisterous bedroom encounter, as depicted in films produced by Edison, Riley Brothers of Bradford[2], Chard's Vitagraph of Great Portland Street, London[3] and the Lumières (all similarly named, whether in English or French), as well as Paul's *A Favourite Nursery Scene*.

If 'The Sculptor's Surprise' was an example of an exhibitor replacing a film's original title with his own, it could have been Paul's *"You Dirty Boy" Statue Comes to Life*. John Barnes suggests that it may have been inspired by the bronze *Manneken-pis* statue in Brussels of a boy urinating into a fountain bowl.[4] If so, what a surprise Cheetham's audience must have had!

He would have been spoilt for choice for 'The Village Blacksmith'. This topic had been addressed seriously by Edison, the Lumières, Méliès and James Williamson of Hove,[5] and comically by Acres and Paul. But 'The Village Blacksmith' was advertised as 'a 10-minutes' picture', when films typically lasted for a minute or so. Several could have been spliced together on one large reel and separated by short lengths of

---

[2] Riley Bros (Joseph and sons) started manufacturing lantern slides in 1884. After William had seen a Lumière *Cinematographe* in Paris they branched out into film-making *circa* 1898 (Dennis M. Copeland in *Who's Who of Victorian Cinema*)

[3] Chard's Vitagraph operated from 1897 to 1900 (the on-line *HRB Centre for British Film and Television Studies. The London Project, The birth of the film business in London*)

[4] John Barnes. *The Beginnings of the Cinema in England 1894–1901, Volume 2: 1897*, pp. 12, 229

[5] Pharmacist James Williamson would supply G.A. Smith with chemicals for film processing. His 1900 re-enactment *Attack on a China Mission – Blue Jackets to the Rescue* was almost certainly the first film with 'cuts' between shots to denote a race against time (Martin Sopocy in *Who's Who of Victorian Cinema*). Most of it can be viewed on '*Britain on Film*' BFI Player

blank film to extend their duration, or even projected at a slower speed. The actor pulling funny faces while mouthing Longfellow's solemn verses in Paul's film could have been augmented by a synchronized spoken delivery of the poem.

No wonder films about firemen were to become a recurring feature of Silvograph shows, considering an 1897 *Optical Magic Lantern Journal* review of one in which 'the engine dashes down the street towards the audience and appears to come right upon them' and a report about an old lady who 'tried to scramble out, and in doing so knocked over the person behind her in her endeavour to get away from the horses'. If the film billed by Cheetham as 'The Great Fire Film' wasn't a re-run of Edison's *The Burning Stable*, it could have been Paul's 'most exciting' *Turnout of a Fire Brigade*, the Lumières' *Fire Call, London* or their *Firemen* series, in which an appliance leaves the station, personnel get ready, train a hose on the flames and perform a life-saving exercise.

Films about both wrestling and juggling were also on the programme. If 'The Wrestlers' featured unidentified participants, it could have been the Lumières' *Japanese Wrestlers* or the European Blair Company's *Wrestling*.[6] On the other hand, one contestant in Edison's *Wrestling Match* was named as a former champion of New Jersey, and a film by Archer & Sons of Liverpool was claimed to feature 'the wrestling championship of the world'.[7] 'Jugglers with table'

---

[6] The European Blair Camera Company, with offices in Holborn, London and manufacturing facilities at Foot's Cray, Kent was established by American inventor Thomas Henry Blair, one-time supplier of film-stock for Edison Kinetoscopes and later to other early film producers (Deac Rossell in *Who's Who of Victorian Cinema*). They may not have produced the 1898–1899 films attributed to them in Denis Gifford's *The British Film Catalogue Volume 1 Fiction Film, 1895–1994* and *The British Film Catalogue Volume 2 Non-Fiction Film, 1888–1994*

[7] Archer & Sons, mainly manufacturers of magic lanterns and slides, branched out into film and film equipment in 1898 (John Barnes. *The Beginnings of the Cinema in England 1894–1901 Volume Three: 1898*, pp 66, 165)

could have been the Lumières' *Japanese jugglers* if the *Rhyl Journal* advertisement is to be believed; but it is called 'Juggler with table' in the *Record and Advertiser*.

Cheetham's magic lantern was put to good use that evening, with slides of men working on a recent Promenade extension, 'effects' and illustrations for songs. He had engaged the services of 'Society Entertainer' Archie D. Melvin, who performed 'original humorous, musical sketches and character songs' and sang in the style of George Grossmith, renowned exponent of Gilbert & Sullivan baritone roles. A piano supplied locally for Melvin was to travel for his use during a continuation of Cheetham's tour. Among the places visited was overwhelmingly Welsh-speaking Llangefni, on the Isle of Anglesey, where the vernacular was used to advertise his *Arddangosfa o Fyw Arluniau Newydd* (Exhibition of New Living Pictures) in the weekly *Cloriannydd* newspaper. Singled out for praise in the following issue were his Blackburn football film and his lantern slides of a recent railway accident between Conwy and Penmaen-mawr, causing the death of the driver and fireman of a goods train after a storm had destroyed the sea-wall.

May saw Cheetham shooting his first film of the future King George V and Queen Mary, during their north Wales tour as Duke and Duchess of Cornwall and York. The *Colwyn Bay and Welsh Coast Pioneer* reported at length on their visit to Conwy. After a welcome by the Mayor and Town Clerk at the railway station, they travelled by open carriage to the castle, where Cheetham was waiting. His film, lasting for nearly four minutes, has survived. At the 'Present Arms' by a military guard-of-honour, the royal carriage sweeps into view and halts facing the camera. Duke, Duchess and two male companions alight, and dozens of guests stream past. The second part of the film starts with the royal carriage reversing into position after the castle visit. Duke, Duchess and party climb aboard and are driven away.

One brief paragraph in the *Pioneer* mentions Cheetham's use of a film 200 feet long for the Conwy film '[which he] intends to exhibit … at Rhyl shortly'. He did so at the Town Hall on Whit Monday, some three weeks later. By then the number of venues visited on tour had risen to between 60 and 70. He must have dispensed with the services of Archie Melvin, since Madame Rose alone provided the live entertainment.

Apart from the Conwy film and 'snap-shots' (lantern slides) of that year's May Day procession, all eight 'new pictures' advertised were comic ones – portraying situations and characters as diverse as a lovers' tryst, fractious infants, marital infidelity, undeserved charity, the perils of fishing, a mischievous ghost, unruly pupils and bill-posters (authorised or unauthorized).

If 'The Soldier's Courtship' was Paul's 1896 production of the same name, Cheetham's audience would see a 'lady of maturer years' attempting to join an amorous pair on a bench and being ejected unceremoniously. In his 1898 re-make entitled *Tommy Atkins in the Park*, open countryside has replaced the original wall in the background, the 'maturer' person approaches through shrubbery and the young lady is a pram-pushing nursemaid.

'Children at Tea' appears to have been either Paul's *The Twins' Tea Party* of 1896 about two little girls quarrelling over a piece of cake or his 1898 re-make. Either way, result: tears.

The title 'The Husband & Servant caught by the Wife' says more about another comic film than its published one, whether Smith's *Hanging Out the Clothes* or Paul's *Mistress and Maid*. Whichever version Cheetham chose, wife is seen discovering husband and servant canoodling behind a sheet on the line and administering appropriate punishment.

The (?) in the title 'The Lame (?) Beggar' suggests that all is not as it seems. If it was Edison's *The Fake Beggar*, the trickster would be seen feigning blindness as well as lameness. He is exposed when he retrieves a proffered coin which has missed his collecting-hat on the pavement but escapes a policeman's clutches in the ensuing chase.

'Troubles of an Angler' must surely feature a soaking to be adjudged comic. Several films come to mind. *The Fisherman's Mishap* was classed as 'humorous' by its distributor, the Warwick Trading Company.[8] *A Fishing Catastrophe* was one of seven comedies produced by the Cinematograph Company.[9] And the 'desciple [sic] of Isaak Walton' in Edison's *The Lone Fisherman* 'catches a ducking and loses both his tackel [sic] and his temper' when the plank he is sitting on is upset.

Of the other three comedies advertised, Smith's *Photographing a Ghost* alone involves trick-photography. Two men carry a large box labeled 'ghost' into a photographer's studio. Proprietor reluctantly opens it, and a transparent apparition steps out. It keeps on disappearing and reappearing. After proprietor attacks it with a chair, it finally collapses through the floor.

Paul's *When the Cat's away the Mice will play* is set in a schoolroom. When the 'cat' (teacher, who else?) is called out, the 'mice' misbehave and discover a tell-tale bottle and glass. 'Cat' returns and (as Paul's catalogue puts it) 'routs' them.

---

[8] The Warwick Trading Company's name was derived from their address in Warwick Court, London. They soon gained prominence as producers of documentary, news and travel films

[9] The Cinematograph Company, active in 1898, also produced films of music-hall acts (Denis Gifford. *British Film Catalogue Volume 1 Fiction Film, 1895–1994*, p. 8)

'The Billposters' Dispute' suggests a conflict over advertising space, whether in Paul's *Rival Bill-stickers* or Méliès's *Défense d'afficher / Post no Bills*. One of Paul's bill-stickers is authorised, while the other is a fly-poster. The brush-wielding operatives in *Défense* complete their tasks without difficulty, even though the prohibition is prominently displayed and seemingly enforced by a sentry.

Cheetham's Conwy film was given further Rhyl Town Hall airings on two successive June evenings, augmented by 'Football Match at Blackburn, the longest Football Film in the World'. His *Journal* advertisement (wrongly dated 'MONDAY and TUESDAY, July 26th and 27th) mentions 'a host of the finest Comic Pictures ever seen' but does not name them. Illustrated songs were sung by his ever-obliging wife.

His next excursion into film-making followed in late July. It featured one of Rhyl's seasonal attractions: the Merrie Men concert party. After he had provided them with limelight illumination for their foreshore pitch, their evening shows were patronised by hundreds, benefiting shop assistants and others busy during the day.

The Merrie Men had started the 1899 season with 16 'Star and Refined Artistes'. They hailed from Dublin, Edinburgh, Manchester, Oldham, Blackburn, Burnley, Leeds, Stafford, Birmingham, London, Brighton and Chichester, with the immediate locality being represented by a 'Comedian Female Impersonator', a 'Character Comedian & Sketch Artiste' and proprietor E.H. Williams as 'Interlocutor and Elocutionist'. Dancer Fred Egan was later joined by newcomer Jimmy Charters to perform a 'double dance'. In his 1900 song-book

Williams was to insist: 'Ladies and Children can safely patronise these entertainments as only the most refined Songs, Jokes and Sketches will be permitted'.[10]

The Merrie Men featured in two films shot by Cheetham on the last Thursday of July: a dance by Egan and Charters and a comic sketch entitled *The School*. They were screened at the Town Hall on the following Monday and Tuesday. In *A Double Dance*, the participants go through their paces to the accompaniment of a variety of instruments. They dance in unison, continually turning towards the audience, to left and to right. The 'teacher' in *The School* chases one troublesome pupil around the 'classroom' several times, applying liberal thwackings on his hands and amply-padded backside. Finally, pupil sits triumphantly on a chair atop a table while his fellows dance around him and exit *stage centre*. Two versions of the Merrie Men films have survived (as listed at the end of this chapter and described in Chapter 16).

On those two summer evenings, Cheetham also screened his Conwy film, 'the longest [Blackburn?] football film in the world', one featuring 'a shoeing smith at work' (a legacy of January's '10-minutes' picture'?), comedies and 'The Great Fire Scene'. While the latter could have been a re-run of an earlier offering, three new films distributed by Warwick had become available. In *Metropolitan Fire Brigade Turn Out* horse-drawn appliances rush along the road, followed by excited onlookers. *The Brighton Fire: Arrival of the Brigade*, shot by G.A. Smith, features a public practice. But the two-part *Fire Call and Rescue* was no mere 'interest' film. A passer-by hears cries from an upper window, notices smoke and raises the alarm. While the firemen rescue the occupants, a 'humorous incident' occurs: water from a hose is accidentally directed at

---

[10] Merrie Men song-book: Flintshire Record Office (ref B.P. 529)

some of the personnel. Needless to say, Madame Rose Garton augmented this wide-ranging programme of filmic fare with her usual illustrated songs.

After ten seasons at Rhyl, Arthur Cheetham was granted a benefit concert at the Town Hall in September. His contributions to the evening's entertainment were the song *The Little Hero* ('by request') and coloured slides of 'Picturesque Wales'. He was supported by his wife, the Merrie Men and 'Professor' Frank Sinclair. The programme also included two films he had taken the previous week: the crowd leaving the Merrie Men show and children on the beach. In the latter (which has survived) two boys engage in a good-natured wrestling bout, boatmen row to shore, other children paddle and adults stroll along the water's edge. Also screened was Birt Acres's 'new picture of the charge of the 12th Lancers at Aldershot'. It may have featured men who had served under 'Sirdar' Kitchener in the Sudan, since an advertisement in *The Era* claims that audiences 'will understand what the Dervishes had to encounter … They charge right at you'.

Arthur Cheetham produced considerably fewer films in 1899 than in 1898. But three depicting the pleasures of holiday Rhyl and one featuring the royals he was to film on two further occasions survive.

Films mentioned in this chapter which can be viewed on *YouTube*: *Sirdar's Reception at Guildhall* (Paul), *Making Sausages (1897)* (Smith), *Pillow Fight – 1897* (Edison), *Bataille d'oreillers (No. 2)* (Lumière), *A Favourite Nursery Scene* (Paul), *New Blacksmith Shop (1895)* (Edison), *Les Forgerons / Blacksmith Scene* (Lumière), *Tommy Atkins in the Park* (Paul),

The Twins' Tea Party (Paul), *Hanging Out the Clothes* (Smith), *The Lone Fisherman 1896* (Edison) and *Défense d'afficher / Post no Bills* (Méliès)

On '*Britain on Film*' *BFI Player*: *E.H. Williams's Merrie Men: Double Dance and 'The School' sketch* (Cheetham) and *Metropolitan Fire Brigade Turn Out* (distributed by the Warwick Trading Company)

On *BFI Screenonline 1890s Films*: *Brighton Fire: Arrival of the Brigade* (Smith, distributed by the Warwick Trading Company)

On *BFI Screenonline 1890s Films*: another version of *E.H. Williams's Merrie Men*, with *The School* ending before the final 'exit *stage centre*' and extended footage of the Double Dance (as explained in Chapter16)

On *Critical Past*: *The Fake Beggar (1898)* (Edison)

Chapter 6

1900: 'new films, just arrived from the Seat of War'

Arthur Cheetham shot no films in 1900. But the war in South
Africa against the Boers of the Orange Free State and Transvaal
republics kept him well supplied. Nearly half of those he
advertised for his Rhyl Town Hall shows on two February
evenings were 'new films just arrived from the Seat of War'.
Although the programme also included lantern slides of the
conflict, it had its lighter side in the form of what were
described as 'many amusing scenes' as well as 'Flashes of Fun'
by ventriloquist Walter Roselle and his 'Famous Family of Five
Funny Folk' (presumably a set of 'talking' dummies). Songs
were provided by both Cheetham and his wife.

Scores of films had been taken at Southampton in 1899 of
troopships bound for South Africa, and two from October
were screened. In the Warwick Trading Company's *The "Roslin
Castle" (Troopship) Leaving for South Africa*, the audiences
would have seen a crowd of well-wishers 'vigorously waving
hats, handkerchiefs, umbrellas, &c.' as the vessel steamed past
with 1,700 troops swarming the decks and rigging. The film of
the *Dunottar Castle* could have been either Warwick's *General
Buller Embarking on the "Dunottar Castle" at Southampton, for
South Africa* or Fuerst's *Sir Redvers Buller Embarking*.
Incidentally, 24-year-old Winston Churchill, correspondent of
the *Morning Post*, was a passenger on the *Dunottar Castle*.

Two films which really had come from 'the Seat of War'
were *Troops Crossing the Modder River by Train* and *Lancers
Crossing the Modder River*. The Modder formed part of the

border between the British Cape Colony and the Orange Free State. The railway bridge spanning it had been destroyed by the Boers in November 1899, but it was soon replaced by British army engineers with a temporary structure. Both films were taken days later by camera-man John Benett-Stanford for Warwick. The soldiers in *Troops Crossing* are Seaforth Highlanders riding in coal-trucks, and the train is protected by an armoured car. Those in *Lancers Crossing* are returning from a military engagement.

The Boers had been the better prepared at the start, making incursions into British territory and laying siege to the strategic railway towns of Kimberley, Ladysmith and Mafeking. But the tide had turned in the new year with the replacement of Buller as C-in-C by Lord Roberts, supported by his deputy Lord Kitchener. Cheetham's audiences would have known that the reinforcements sent included ten Rhyl volunteers who had received a mere week's training at Wrexham prior to embarkation. They did not all return.

Camera-men faced danger in the pursuit of realism during the war, as in the case of Warwick's Joseph Rosenthal at Pretoria in June 1900. The catalogue entry for his film explains: 'Little clouds of dust are thrown up constantly by the enemy's bullets striking the ground … Boer shells were bursting all around and overhead'. But the absence of a well-defined 'front line' made it difficult to film more than troop movements and military installations. Consequently, some producers emulated Méliès's *actualités reconstituées*. Paul engaged a retired officer with eighteen years' active service in the Transvaal to help him shoot 'reproductions of the principal incidents of the war' on a golf course near London in late 1899 'to meet the demand for something more exciting'. He was quite forthcoming about their origin and doubled the charge made to exhibitors from the usual sixpence per foot to a shilling 'owing to the number of men engaged and the enormous expense'. Cheetham screened Paul's *Capture of a Maxim Gun by the British*, which featured the machine-gun invented by Sir Hiram Maxim. The film advertised as 'British Attack on a Boer Outpost' appears to be Acres's 'reproduction' *The Rifle Brigade driving in an enemy outpost* about British soldiers forcing opponents from trenches at bayonet-point.

The *Journal* advertisement sardonically describes one film as showing 'How British Tars [sailors] serve the Enemy'. If shot *en route* to battle, it could have been *Naval 4.7 Gun* by Col Walter Beevor RAMC for Paul, showing one of these weapons being hauled by forty bullocks. But if set in the comparative calm of a practice-ground, perhaps it was Warwick's *Bluejackets' Field Gun Drill at Durban*, portraying teams of sailors dismantling, transporting and reassembling guns ready for firing (an exercise later known as the Naval Field Gun Run, which inspired a Royal Tournament contest between 1907 and 1999). Incidentally, '4.7' refers to the diameter in inches of the shells fired.

To complete the list of films advertised for those two February evenings: *Charge of the 12th Lancers* may have been the Acres film shot at Aldershot and screened by Cheetham at his 1899 benefit concert. If so, the headlong rush towards the camera would harmonise with the Boer War fare offered.

Cheetham then toured to over 25 Welsh towns and returned to Rhyl Town Hall on Whit Monday with 'all the latest war films'. Rhyl folk would have read about the surrender of Boer General Piet Cronje in the local press. The *Record and Advertiser* for 3 March had carried Lord Roberts's dispatch to the War Office: 'Paardeberg 7.45.a.m., 27th February. General Cronje and all his forces capitulated unconditionally at daylight this morning and he is now a prisoner in my camp'. But if the audience were expecting to see a formal ceremony in *Cronje's Surrender to Lord Roberts*, they would have been disappointed. Taken for Paul by Beevor, it merely shows the Boer leader being escorted by cavalry in a horse-drawn wagon across a featureless plain. Paul's catalogue observes: 'As the cart passes the camera, Cronje is seen to look out in astonishment at it'. The general was to be held prisoner on St Helena until the peace negotiations of 1902.

4.7 guns were much-filmed weapons, whether on arrival in port (as in Warwick's *Landing the 4.7-inch Naval Guns at Port Elizabeth*), being transported across country (as in Beevor's *Naval 4.7 Gun* mentioned above) or in battle. The film Cheetham called 'The 4.7 in. gun in action' could have been Benett-Stanford's *The Big 4.7 Inch Naval Gun in action at Modder River Engagement Firing One Shell*. The enemy fire was claimed to be so hot that the camera-man was compelled to retire.

The Maxim machine-gun delivered 500 rounds per minute and is claimed to have been the weapon most associated with British imperial conquest. But the February screening of *Capture of a Maxim Gun by the British* indicates that it was being supplied to both sides. So Cheetham's Whit Monday audience must have been pleased with 'Jack Tars with Maxim Gun'. It may have been the Paul 'reproduction' called *Battle of Glencoe*, in which actors play British sailors 'storming the hill, and driving the Boers over the ridge with a Maxim and a strong rifle fire'.

Care of the wounded featured in 'reproductions' produced by both Paul and Edison. In the former's *Nurses on the Battlefield*, 'wounded' and 'dead' lie on the ground; a stretcher party, a doctor, an orderly and nurses tend a Boer; and a British soldier is carried in for attention. In the latter's *Red Cross Ambulance on Battlefield in Boer War* a surgeon directs an ambulance corps, who 'tenderly ... pick up the unfortunates and place them in the ambulance'. However, the film unambiguously billed by Cheetham as 'Hospital Corps picking up wounded at Modder Bridge' resonates better with Benett-Stanford's *The Ambulance Corps at Work*, showing at that very location how 'the many wounded lying on the battlefield were picked up by this splendid Ambulance Corps who dash from one to the other, carrying and depositing the men in the ten-mule ambulance'.

The programme also included 'portraits [lantern slides] of all the leading generals at the front', including Baden Powell, 'the hero of Mafeking'. Live entertainment was provided by Madame Rose Garton and the Sisters Trescott with their solos and duets on the auto-harp.

The lifting of the Boers' seven-month siege of Mafeking ten days before Cheetham's Whit Monday show had engendered widespread expressions of patriotism. In Rhyl, according to the *Journal*, the majority were snugly indoors when the reports of (lifeboat?) rockets aroused them. Some rushed to the streets and heard 'Mafeking is relieved' on all sides. Others were unconvinced, even by the telegram displayed at the Post Office. But 'enthusiasm excited enthusiasm' when the bells of St Thomas's Church 'burst forth into joyous melodies' and the Town Hall bell 'began clanging hideously'.

Flags appeared on buildings as if by magic. Cyclists and pedestrians paraded through the streets to a cacophony of noise created by horns, trays, biscuit tins etc. While councillors addressed a crowd from the Town Hall balcony, the people hurrahed, tins were banged and the gathering burst into *God Save the Queen*. Bonfires and coloured lights lit up the Promenade. The town band arrived. Parading resumed and continued until midnight: bicycles illuminated by Chinese lanterns, children carrying lighted lanterns and dogs fleeing the noise or joining in the general din. Then the band played *Auld Lang Syne*, and the crowd dispersed.

That was just Saturday! Celebrations continued throughout the weekend, culminating in a bonfire and fireworks on the Monday evening. What a curtain-raiser for Cheetham's Whit Monday show! Lord Roberts's entry into Pretoria on the Tuesday was the signal for more festivities.

Winston Churchill survived the ambush of an armoured train, was imprisoned in a PoW camp but eventually escaped. He enlisted as an NCO and was among the first British troops to enter Ladysmith and Pretoria. He returned to England on the *Dunottar Castle*. Not everyone in Britain approved of the war. David Lloyd George was a notable opponent. The 1918 film *The Life Story of David Lloyd George* includes his celebrated speech at Birmingham and his escape from an angry crowd disguised as a policeman. It was withdrawn in suspicious circumstances soon after production, disappeared for 76 years, was discovered and was painstakingly conserved by the National Screen and Sound Archive of Wales. It is available in DVD form from the National Library of Wales.

Films mentioned in this chapter which can be viewed on British Pathé's *Boer War Material, reel 2: The "Roslin Castle" (Troopship) Leaving for South Africa; General Buller Embarking on the "Dunottar Castle" at Southampton, for South Africa;*

Troops Crossing the Modder River by Train and *Lancers Crossing the Modder River* (all by the Warwick Trading Company) as well as other Boer War films

On *YouTube*: *Cronje's Surrender to Lord Roberts* (Paul) and *Red Cross Ambulance on Battlefield in Boer War* (Edison)

On *BFI Screenonline 1890s Films*: *Bluejackets' Field Gun Drill at Durban (1898)* (the Warwick Trading Company)

Also on *YouTube*, but not mentioned in the chapter: *Royal Naval Field Gun Competition 1999*. For comparison with *Bluejackets' Field Gun Drill at Durban (1898)*

Chapter 7

1901: 'palpably offside'

Returning from a tour of 86 towns, Arthur Cheetham hired Rhyl Town Hall on Whit Monday and Tuesday 1901 to screen a varied programme of topicals, travel films, dramatic reconstructions, comedies and 'a most thrilling picture entitled "Saved from the Fire"'. But his newspaper advertisements gave pride of place to a return visit of Walter Roselle and his Five Funny Folk, the ever-faithful Madame Rose Garton and the Rhyl debut of 11-year-old boy pianist Gus Cheetham. He was to play musical-comedy and operatic selections 'during the display of animated pictures ... and various [magic lantern] views'.

One of the topicals, featuring a Rhyl v Wrexham football match, was listed immediately below Roselle, Madame Rose and Cheetham Jr in the advertisements. Both teams were playing in a competition called 'The Combination', which had originated in the Liverpool/Manchester area. The other clubs participating during the 1900-01 season were Newton-le-Willows, Oswestry, Tranmere Rovers, Warrington, White Star Wanderers and Hudson's of Liverpool, together with Bangor, Buckley and Chirk in north Wales.

Rhyl and Wrexham had met twice that season: at Rhyl just before Christmas and at Wrexham in February. The journalistic treatment of both matches was decidedly partisan. Commenting on the December encounter (won 2-1 by Rhyl), *Record and Advertiser* columnist 'The Chiel' failed to understand why a third Rhyl attempt at goal was disallowed.

And he declared Wrexham's sole scorer to be 'palpably offside'. Wrexham won the return match 3-0, and the *Wrexham Advertiser* observed that 'J. Owens [of Wrexham], only having the goal keeper to contend with, was deliberately fouled just as he was going to shoot'. This victory took Wrexham to the top of the table, and that is where they were at the end of the season (with Rhyl second). It is not clear which match featured in the film, since it was advertised as 'Rhyl v. Wrexham' in the *Record and Advertiser* and 'Wrexham v. Rhyl' in the *Journal*. Nor is there any indication as to who shot it. Had Cheetham been responsible, it would be surprising that he didn't claim the credit.

Royalty featured in the programme. 'Royal Review in Phœnix Park', shot during Queen Victoria's visit to Dublin in 1900, was viewed by Cheetham's Whit-week audiences thirteen months after the event. Other places would have fared better. For example: in his *Came the Dawn*, Cecil Hepworth relates how he had rushed the negatives of his Dublin footage by boat and train to his Walton-on-Thames studio. Prints were produced the following day, shown in London that evening and posted to Dublin and other major cities 'so that the loyal inhabitants of Britain were able to follow the movements of their Queen in the Emerald Isle very shortly after the chief ceremonies connected with her visit had closed'. Although the Queen's visit had been covered by six English film-makers, Paul and Williamson alone recorded the Phœnix Park review. If Cheetham had screened Paul's, his audiences would have seen Victoria look directly at the camera from her carriage.

Hepworth's *Return of Lord Roberts* featured the former C-in-C in South Africa after he had yielded command to Kitchener. He reached the Solent on 2 January 1901 and proceeded to the royal residence at Osborne on the Isle of

Wight to be admitted into the Order of Merit by the Queen. On the following day he was welcomed at Southampton and travelled by train to Paddington, where the Prince and Princess of Wales met him for a triumphal ride to Buckingham Palace. He returned to Osborne on the 14th for his elevation to an earldom at what was to be the last audience given by the Queen. *Return of Lord Roberts* captured his arrival at Southampton and the drive to the Palace. Although feted as a hero, Roberts had suffered the loss of his only son during the South African war. One poignant verse of an anonymous poem published in the *Rhyl Journal* contrasts public acclaim with private grief: 'Our gallant Queen will give we know, / All honour due to thee, / But honour and gold will never bring / Thy loved one back to thee'.

The Queen died on 22 January. Her funeral procession at Cowes, the royal yacht carrying the coffin past warships firing salutes in the Solent, the arrival at Portsmouth, the procession through London, the arrival by train at Windsor, the procession through the town and scenes outside St George's Chapel were covered variously by nine companies in a total of over 40 films. But whatever was the content of 'Queen Victoria's Funeral' screened by Cheetham three months later, it must surely have featured the gun-carriage carrying the flag-draped coffin surmounted by crown, orb and sceptre.

One topical film recalled a dramatic event of the Wednesday before Whit-week involving royalty, albeit informally. Presumably arriving too late to be advertised in the local papers, it was reported in the following week's *Journal* as showing 'the wreck of the Shamrock II, with the King on board, and Shamrock I coming to the rescue'. Both craft were racing yachts owned by Sir Thomas Lipton, of humble Glasgow origins but by then a millionaire tea importer, grocery-chain owner and friend of royalty. Between 1899 and 1930, he spent lavishly but fruitlessly on five successive *Shamrocks* to compete in the annual *America's Cup* races held off the US east coast near New York. On the fateful Wednesday *Shamrocks I* and *II* had been in a race during Cowes Week, held on the Solent. A sudden squall struck both vessels broadside, and *Shamrock II* was damaged most. Having been informed that no-one was injured, King Edward, aboard *Shamrock II*, responded phlegmatically by lighting up a second cigar! Both Warwick and Paul had filmed the regatta and the damage to *Shamrock II*. So Cheetham could have chosen either version of what the *Journal* called 'the wreck of the Shamrock II ... '. Incidentally, she was eventually repaired in time to compete in that year's *America's Cup* races.

Although films of the on-going South African war were screened on those two evenings, the inclusion of 'Street Scene in Pekin' and two dramatic reconstructions was an indication that China was becoming a major theatre of interest. Warwick had sent camera-men there, as well as to Korea and Japan. The emphasis in their *Street Scene in the Tartar City* was, as their catalogue explained, on dirt, smells and unpaved streets. But if Cheetham had obtained a copy of E.F.G. Hatch's *Street Scene in Pekin*, his audiences would have enjoyed the globe-trotting MP's record of 'the quaint conveyances and traffic of a purely native quarter, including a drove of camels'.

Britain, France, Germany, Russia, the USA and Japan had been granted permission to open ports, establish banks and develop railways, telegraphs and mining in China. But they were vehemently opposed by a militant organisation dubbed 'The Boxers' because of their devotion to fisticuffs and gymnastics. They aimed to destroy everything they considered foreign, slaughtering Christian missionaries and anyone suspected of favouring western ideas. Legations were attacked, diplomats were killed and the survivors sought refuge in the British Legation. It was besieged but eventually relieved by an international force.

In the absence of films of actual conflict, Cheetham was indebted to Blackburn-based Mitchell & Kenyon for their dramatic reconstructions entitled *Attack on a Mission Station* and *Attempted Capture of an English Nurse and Children,* shot in the countryside near their hometown. In the former, lasting for a minute and a half, Boxers chase a missionary's wife and daughter home. Missionary bundles them inside, fells one intruder with a chair and barricades the door. They are all dragged out but are saved by the timely arrival of British marines. In the shorter *Attempted Capture* an English army officer passes a girl and a nurse tending a baby. Nurse places her charge on the ground. A Boxer appears, picks baby up, flings it at her feet and drags her to the ground. He is joined by his fellows, one of whom carries the baby away while the others start tying girl and nursemaid up. But officer hears nurse's screams and alerts his soldiers, who pursue Boxers, firing as they run. He then returns baby to grateful nurse.[1]

Among the comic films screened, trick-photography figured large in Paul's *The Haunted Curiosity Shop.* Its proprietor is plagued by a succession of ghostly visitors, ending with three gnomes who jump out of a large jar and coalesce before being popped back in. Flames, smoke and an enormous head emerge

---

[1] Little was known about Sagar Mitchell and James Kenyon until 1994, when local historian Peter Worden discovered the negatives of about 800 of their comedies, dramas, interest films and topicals shot mainly in the North of England. Together with Robin Whalley, he produced the original catalogue of the collection (Vanessa Toulmin. *Electric Edwardians, The Story of the Mitchell & Kenyon Collection,* pp. 1, 2 *et seq*)

Cheetham's foreshore stand
(author's collection)

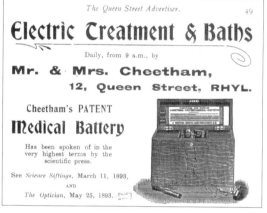

Cheetham's medical battery,
advertised in his Rhyl Pilot,
1903
(Flintshire Record Office, ref
D/DM/919.44)

Rhyl beach: a photograph by Arthur Cheetham in J.D. Polkinghorne's
Bracing Rhyl, 1900 *(author's collection)*

i

The first Kinetoscope Parlor

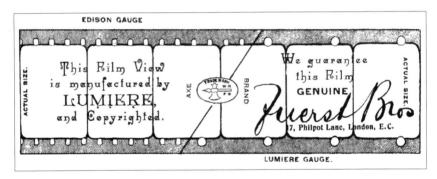

'Edison' and 'Lumière' perforations compared

Holiday Rhyl, circa 1900: *Promenade, minstrel pitch and audience on beach,*
Grand Pavilion and Bijou Pavilion on pier
(Rhyl Library, Museum & Arts Centre)

Rhyl Palace Theatre and Summer Gardens (the late John K. Parker)

Rhyl Town Hall: a photograph by John Williams, Rhyl in J.D. Polkinghorne's Bracing Rhyl, 1900 *(author's collection)*

32-year-old Arthur Cheetham as Captain of Rhyl Cycling Club's first ladies' tour, May 1897 (National Screen and Sound Archive of Wales based at the National Library of Wales)

iii

Advertisement for a bi-unial magic lantern in The Art of Projection and Complete Magic Lantern Manual, *1893*

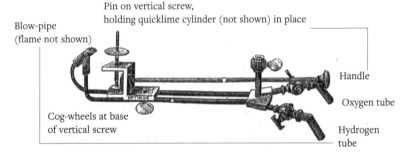

A Limelight Jet. The oxygen/hydrogen flame heats the quicklime cylinder. Turning the handle rotates and raises it by means of the cog-wheels and the vertical screw

From Cheetham's Holyhead Mail Boat, *1898 (author's collection)*

From Cheetham's Blackburn Rovers v West Bromwich Albion, *1898*
(*author's collection*)

From Cheetham's Royal Visit to Conway, *1899: Prince alights from carriage*
(*author's collection*)

From Cheetham's E. H. Williams's Merrie Men: Double Dance, *1899*
(author's collection)

From Cheetham's E. H. Williams's Merrie Men: 'The School' sketch, *1899:*
'pupils' sit obediently (author's collection)

From Cheetham's film of children on Rhyl beach, 1899
(author's collection)

Rhyl Royal Alexandra Children's Hospital and Convalescent Home,
destination of the 1902 royal visit filmed by Cheetham
(lantern slide from the collection of the late Eric Foulkes)

Rhyl High Street decorated for the 1902 royal visit filmed by Cheetham (lantern slide from the collection of the late Eric Foulkes)

From Cheetham's Children leaving Christ Church Schools, Rhyl, 1902: *boy looks camera in lens (author's collection)*

From Cheetham's Children leaving the National Schools, Rhyl, 1902: *boys play leapfrog (author's collection)*

From Cheetham's
The 1903 May Day
Procession in Rhyl:
Rhyl Fire Brigade
(author's collection)

From Cheetham's
Buffalo Bill's visit to
Rhyl, 1903: *Cody*
alights from carriage
(author's collection)

From Cheetham's Rhyl Cycling Club outing to Nant Hall, Prestatyn, 1903:
well-dressed ladies smile at his camera (National Screen and Sound Archive
of Wales based at the National Library of Wales)

Proclamation ceremony of Rhyl's 1904 National Eisteddfod, 1903. Cheetham may have filmed it. Rhyl Record and Advertiser, *8 August 1903 (Flintshire Record Office)*

Cheetham's Rhyl cinema, 1909. Large poster on left advertises a film of Blériot's cross-channel flight; smaller one in window features his monoplane (Ian Meyrick)

Cheetham's Rhyl cinema today
(author's collection)

Cheetham's Aberystwyth cinema in 'talkies' days, as indicated by the B T-H
(British Thomson-Houston) sound-system sign (Ceredigion Record Office)

Cheetham's Colwyn Bay cinema today (author's collection)

Colwyn Bay Public Hall today
(author's collection)

*Cheetham's Cheetham Hill
Road cinema today
(photograph by David
Eve)*

From Cheetham's film of the 1907 'Signboard' affair

Ladders and pole at the ready (author's collection)

Audience leaving cinema (author's collection)

*'THE BOARD ABOVE ...' poster being pasted onto the cinema wall
(author's collection)*

*Rhyl's Queen's Palace during the 1907 fire, filmed by Cheetham (lantern side
from the collection of the late Eric Foulkes)*

The Pavilion Theatre on Rhyl Promenade. Cheetham filmed work in progress there twice in 1908 (picture postcard, author's collection)

From Cheetham's 1908 film Sunny Rhyl First Stop *(National Screen and Sound Archive of Wales based at the National Library of Wales)*

Blériot monoplane, as used by Vivian Hewitt when filmed by Cheetham in 1912 (Dunlop Rubber Company)

Christmas lantern slide. Seated (left to right): Mrs Cheetham, Arthur Cheetham and Gwen (later Mrs Cordery); standing: Bernard, Edith, Gustavus and Frances (from the collection of the late Eric Foulkes)

From Marriage of G. A. Cheetham and Miss E. M. Lawson, 1913: *Rhyl's pioneer film-maker filmed (author's collection)*

From the film attributable to Cheetham about boys upsetting a market trader's cart: visitor asks directions (author's collection)

from the jar. Finally, proprietor flees in terror as the head fills the screen as if to swallow the audience.

The comedy about an unfortunate fisherman could have been Gibbons' Bio-Tableaux's *Fisherman's Luck* or Edison's of the same name. After Gibbons's lone fisherman is pulled into the water, a rescuer dives in after him. The action is then reversed, by re-shooting the pulling-in and the diving-in with the camera held upside-down and adding the result (right-way up) to the initial footage.[2] Edison's film features a pair of fishermen. They both fall in, but one of them must save the other after they are ignored by the occupants of a passing rowing-boat.

Cheetham's screening of 'Saved from the Fire' indicates the continuing popularity of films about fire-fighting with his audiences. New ones by Paul and Hepworth would have become available by the Whit-week of 1901. Paul's *Plucked from the Burning* is set in a bedroom. A mother and her child are awakened by smoke and are beaten back by flames at the door. But a fireman enters through a window and rescues them before the ceiling collapses. The title of Hepworth's *The Burning Stable* is reminiscent of Edison's earlier production of the same name but it was longer and more action-filled. Not only are horses, carts, carriages etc removed to safety, but firemen also direct a stream of water on the flames.

There is no record of Arthur Cheetham shooting films in 1901. However, when he returned to Rhyl Town Hall in mid-January 1902, unidentified 'New Local Pictures' were on the programme. But their dates and locations remain a mystery.

---

[2] Gibbons' Bio-Tableaux, productive between 1898 and 1901, was owned by music-hall magnate Sir Walter Gibbons (Barry Anthony in *Who's Who of Victorian Cinema*)

Films mentioned in this chapter which can be viewed on *YouTube*: *Queen Victoria's Funeral (1901)* (BFI, shot at various locations), *Fisherman's Luck* (Edison) and nearly all of *The Haunted Curiosity Shop* (Paul)

On '*Britain on Film*' *BFI Player*, but not mentioned in the chapter: most of *Attack on a China Mission – Blue Jackets to the Rescue* (Williamson, a 'Boxers' dramatic reconstruction)

Chapter 8

1902: *Royalty and Schoolchldren*

This chapter's title gives an indication of the content of the three local films shot by Arthur Cheetham in 1902: a brief royal visit to the town and pupils emerging from school. But for two evenings in January, he hired Rhyl Town Hall to screen films advertised: 'as shown in the Great Albert Hall, Sheffield, in September last' (presumably on his annual tour). Among them were 'Return of the Duke and Duchess of Cornwall and York', 'A Sensational Ride on the front of an Express Engine' and the unidentified 'New Local Pictures' mentioned at the end of Chapter 7. Projected on a 16-foot-wide screen, they were to be 'the largest yet shown in Rhyl'. Live entertainment was provided by Madame Rose Garton with her illustrated songs, son Gus on the piano and the first appearance of Will Hunter, billed as a ventriloquial humorist.

The Duke and Duchess's homecoming from an Empire tour in November 1901 on board *SS Ophir* had been covered by five English production companies. Among the films that Cheetham could choose from were Warwick's *S.S. Ophir entering Portsmouth Harbour*, Hepworth's *Arrival of the Ophir and Departure by Train from Portsmouth* and Paul's *London's Reception to the Royal Travellers*.

'A Sensational Ride on the front of an Express Engine' was a 'phantom ride' film – groundbreaking in those days of static cameras, since they were shot typically from the front of a moving train. The American Mutoscope & Biograph's 70mm-gauge *The Haverstraw Tunnel* of 1897 (which Cheetham could not have screened) was one of the earliest, filmed in the

Hudson Valley, north of New York. An *Era* review of its screening at London's Palace Theatre of Varieties observed that the viewer became 'part and parcel of the picture ... tearing along at express speed on a cow-catcher, with the landscape simply leaping towards him'. By early 1902, Cheetham had about 30 UK-produced 35mm phantom rides to choose from. The unattributed 1899 *Ride on an Express Engine* may have been among them. It transports the audience vicariously along a cutting, under a bridge, through a tunnel and out at the other end – all in less than a minute.

Cheetham had been entertaining audiences with gramophone records for some years. But this time a 'Giant Concert-phone' was to play not only musical selections but also his own recordings of the Penrhyn Male Voice Choir made recently at Rhyl. The choir had been singing at the Town Hall during the previous week in aid of the families suffering from the long-running strike at their Bethesda slate-quarry. 'Come and hear ... "Tôn y Botel" ' was Cheetham's exhortation about their rendition of the popular hymn-tune in his *Journal* advertisement. Fortuitously, the anecdotal story of its discovery in a bottle washed up on a beach in the Llŷn Peninsula had appeared in the *Daily Mail* two days before the choir's Rhyl appearance. Also to be played on the concert-phone was his record of the choir singing the Welsh National Anthem *Hen Wlad fy Nhadau* 'as a solo and chorus'.

Soon after returning from their Empire tour the Duke and Duchess of Cornwall and York had become Prince and Princess of Wales. They were to visit Rhyl in May 1902 to open an extension to the town's Royal Alexandra Children's Hospital and Convalescent Home. The institution's name dated from 1894 when, as Princess Alexandra, the Prince's mother, had laid its foundation stone. The 1902 visit, although a source of great pride to townsfolk, was but an adjunct to other engagements in north Wales, such as the Prince's installation as Chancellor of the University of Wales at Caernarfon. But following representations on behalf of Rhyl Council, the royal couple had condescended to break their return train journey at Rhyl on the strict understanding that the visit would last no more than an hour.

Cheetham's use of two cameras to film the day's proceedings was reported at length by the *Record and Advertiser*. He started at the railway station, where the Prince and Princess received a VIP welcome. He then rushed to the hospital for the arrival of the procession, where he captured 'several incidents of an interesting character' including 'horses shying at the soldiers'. The arrival of local councillors and their officials was, he considered, 'one of most effective incidents of the day', since they would be shown on the screen 'first in life-size and then in most gigantic proportions as they near and pass the camera'. On the conclusion of the formalities, he filmed the procession leaving and the crowd dispersing.

Then followed a 'great and unexpected novelty – a Phantom Panoramic Ride', with his camera strapped to a rubber-tyred float lent by a local fishmonger. It enabled him to film 'all the decorations along the route, the people viewing the sights, and immense crowds in High Street, overtaking the Chairman and several members of the Council &c. … as seen from the back of the vehicle ... which will give the effect to the audience as if they were seated in [the float] and going along at a very rapid pace'. The film ended with the royal couple's departure at the station, their train disappearing in the distance and the crowd cheering.

Cheetham wasn't the only person to operate a ciné camera

in Rhyl that day. Blackburn's Mitchell & Kenyon also covered the visit. 4½ minutes of their *Royal Visit to Rhyl* have survived, featuring the procession, crowds in the streets and firemen, mounted police and carriages returning to the railway station at the end of the day.

Rhyl children would receive 'elementary' education from five years of age to between 10 and 13 at that time. Whereas the town's 'National' schools (Infants, Boys and Girls) were 'Church of England' (as the Anglican Church was called in Wales before its 1920 disestablishment), the Christ Church 'British' schools were non-denominational. Cheetham shot films outside both buildings during the same week as the royal visit. They have survived.

The *Record and Advertiser's* description of the Christ Church film as 'a happy joyous spectacle of child-life brimming over with youthful enthusiasm and vigour' is no journalistic hyperbole. Wave after wave of boys and girls of all ages emerge through a narrow archway, walking, talking, playing and generally milling around in the street. Miss Adelaide Owen was an Infants teacher there. In 1983, as nonagenarian Mrs Clarke, she recorded her memories of that day. '[Mr Cheetham] must have asked my headmistress if he could take pictures [of pupils] going across the road, and then had she got anybody responsible for keeping them moving', she explained. Those duties were entrusted to young Adelaide, so 'I stood in the gateway for the children to come out. And I did as I was told … kept every child on the go, so there was a constant stream'.

Cheetham's camera captured more than a constant stream. Boys play leapfrog and 'strong horse' (in which a line of them bending over and facing the wall is 'mounted' by an opponent attempting to ensure their collapse). Teachers walk primly out of school. Other adults appear. A variety of hand-carts and horse-drawn vehicles pass by. One boy smiles at the camera and looks it straight in the lens, giving today's viewer the uncanny feeling not so much of watching the past as being watched by it. A chimney-sweep carrying a pair of long-handled brushes talks to some of the boys. He is none other than Adelaide's uncle. As Mrs Clarke, she reminisced: 'While Mr Cheetham was filming, Uncle John came from a job. We'd had a storm, and he'd been on the Parade [Promenade] to, I believe, mend a chimney … I had to keep my mouth shut. I couldn't say "Hello Uncle John"'.

The National Schools film presents a similar succession of pupils, although they tend to walk along the pavement rather more sedately. But one group of boys line up in the road to play leapfrog, seemingly oblivious of approaching horse-drawn carts. Among the passers-by one young man runs towards the camera, flaps his coat-tails in birdlike fashion, jumps in the air and exits *stage right*.

The royal visit film was screened at Rhyl Town Hall throughout Whit-week, augmented on the Thursday, Friday and Saturday by those of the schoolchildren. While the advertisement for the last three evenings in the *Record and Advertiser* describes the National Schools film as 'A Masterpiece in Amateur Photography', it is called 'a veritable masterpiece in **animated** photography' in the *Journal* – surely what Cheetham intended!

Also on the programme that week were several of Cheetham's earlier films, an otherwise undocumented 'A Crowd on Rhyl Parade', 'a splendid selection of comic and miscellaneous pictures' and a 'grand finale of fire pictures'.

Having screened so many films about fire-fighting since at least January 1897, he could have amassed quite a collection. But Warwick's 29-part *Fire Brigade Series* and Williamson's dramatic *Fire!* had become available in late 1901. While the former featured firemen at work in London, Birmingham, Brighton, Bristol etc, the latter was shot at Hove. In it, the alarm is raised, the local brigade spring into action, their horse-drawn appliances rush to the scene and the rescue is shot from both inside and outside the burning house.

Madame Rose Garton was billed as contributing to the week's entertainment, as were Will Hunter (described this time merely as a ventriloquist) and Gus Cheetham (by now 'the famous boy pianist'). The newspaper advertisements also announced that for the first time Cheetham was screening films 'with ELECTRIC LIGHT' – proudly rated as being of '6,000 Candle-power'. Limelight had obviously been dispensed with, at least for his film projector.

King Edward VII was to be crowned at Westminster Abbey on Thursday 26 June. Filming was not permitted. So Georges Méliès, G.A. Smith and Charles Urban of the Warwick Trading Company co-operated on a dramatic reconstruction of the ceremony. The 10-scene *Le Sacre d'Edouard VII / The Coronation of Edward VII* was shot at Méliès's Paris studio before the proposed date of the event (therefore perhaps better described in Méliès terms as an *actualité pré-constituée*). But the King contracted appendicitis, and both coronation and film's release were postponed.

There is no evidence of *Le Sacre d'Edouard VII* ever being screened by Cheetham. But he responded with characteristic initiative to the delay. The *Rhyl Journal* for Saturday 21 June had enthusiastically predicted: 'before another week shall have passed the country will be right in the midst of the Coronation festivities'. Cheetham must have hoped to obtain footage of the processions, since he advertised the following Monday's show in the *Journal* thus: 'Don't go to London to see the Coronation. Save money! Stop in Rhyl! and see it all at the Silvograph Electric Animated Pictures'.

However, not to be frustrated when he heard about the King's illness, he expanded his planned single evening's entertainment to a whole week (with matinees on the Wednesday and the Saturday) and announced boldly in a follow-up advertisement: 'Though the Coronation is Postponed the Exhibition of the SILVOGRAPH Electric Animated Pictures is NOT postponed'. And that in the very issue of the *Journal* that carried a Buckingham Palace bulletin on the King's progress and a cautious prognosis by Rhyl Council Vice-Chairman and GP, Dr Girdlestone!

Nevertheless, Cheetham managed to acquire some coronation-related material, which he advertised as 'The Coronation Review of 30,000 Troops at Aldershot to her Majesty the Queen'. The event had been held on 16 June. The King was indisposed and did not leave the royal pavilion. So he was represented by the Prince of Wales, who rode to the saluting-point for a march-past of rain-soaked foot-soldiers headed by Lord Roberts leading the Cavalry Brigade. The Queen and other lady members of the royal party watched from enclosed carriages. Gifford's *The British Film Catalogue Volume 2 Non-Fiction Film, 1888–1994* lists several films of a Coronation review of Indian and colonial troops by the Prince of Wales at London's Horse Guards Parade in early July. But there is no reference to the Aldershot film. So, like the football film which inspired the cries of 'goal' in 1898, it must remain unidentified.

Once again, Madame Rose Garton shared the stage with Will Hunter, while son Gus's contribution included *The Coronation Prize March*, composed by Percy Godfrey, Master of Music at King's School, Canterbury in a competition for a work to be played during the coronation festivities. Also on the bill were the films that Cheetham had produced that year and 'a magnificent selection of amazing and sensational [but unnamed] comic films', with a change of programme each evening. Cheetham seems to have survived the coronation's postponement in style!

There were no more Silvograph shows at the Town Hall that year, and the annual tour started on 8 September. A 'communication' entitled 'How Rhyl is Advertised Free of Charge' appeared in the *Record and Advertiser* in early November (submitted by guess who!). It reported that in those first nine weeks alone, 32 towns had been visited, including Belper in Derbyshire, several in the Midlands, Evesham, Cirencester and Swindon, as well as Dunstable and Hatfield (some 30 and 20 miles from London respectively). The patronage of Lady Campbell-Bannerman (wife of Liberal leader Sir Henry Campbell-Bannerman) and 'a party of six other County gentry' at Brackley, Northamptonshire is proudly mentioned – as is the presence of schoolboys from 'the best families of gentry from all parts of the country'. Thus: 'the advertising of the Royal Visit to Rhyl will be spread over a very wide area, among the very best class of people, and the attendance of nobility and such a class of people as those mentioned must be very gratifying to Mr Cheetham, and satisfactory to his fellow-townsfolk who desire to see the name of Rhyl brought before the better-class public'. And while Cheetham stayed in Rhyl 'superintending the operations' the tour was 'capably managed' by his wife.

Films mentioned in this chapter which can be viewed on *YouTube*: *Fire!* (Williamson) and nearly four minutes of *Le Sacre d'Edouard VII / The Coronation of Edward VII* (Méliès, Smith and Urban)

On '*Britain on Film*' *BFI Player*: *Children leaving Christ Church Schools, Rhyl; Children leaving the National Schools, Rhyl* (both by Cheetham) and *Royal Visit to Rhyl* (Mitchell & Kenyon)

On *BFI Screenonline 1900s Films*: *Ride on an Express Engine* (an unattributed phantom-ride film)

Chapter 9

1903: *May Day, Buffalo Bill, Outing and Eisteddfod*

The title of this chapter summarises the topics covered by the four films shot by Arthur Cheetham in 1903 – an annual Rhyl event, the visit of an American celebrity, a day out for members of a local organisation close to the film-maker's heart and a foretaste of a national cultural festival to be held in the town. 1903 was also the year when he first advertised a film by the major French company *Pathé Frères*.[1]

He interrupted the 1902-03 tour to appear at Rhyl Town Hall on two evenings in late January. The films listed in his *Journal* advertisement were a pantomime, topicals, another phantom ride, comedies and a music-hall 'turn'. Live entertainment was provided once again by ventriloquist Will Hunter, together with newcomer J.P. Gaunt, comedian and impersonator of the celebrated music-hall performer and pantomime 'dame' Dan Leno.

A 'Grand Pantomime of Ali-Baba! In 12 Magnificent Scenes' was billed as 'the longest picture yet shown in Rhyl'. This Pathé film, lasting for over eight minutes, has not survived, but a 6-scene re-make of similar duration has. It starts with Ali watching thieves enter a cave to deposit their booty. After they have left, he goes in, loads his donkey with the gold

---

[1] Charles Pathé was introduced to film in 1895 by buying replica kinetoscopes from R.W. Paul. In 1896 he and his brother Émile established their *Société Pathé Frères* in Paris, later opening studios in France, other European countries and the USA. They opened a London office in 1902 to distribute their films in the UK (Henri Bousquet in *Who's Who of Victorian Cinema*). Richard Abel's *The Ciné Goes to Town: French Cinema, 1896–1914* refers to their first cinema, opened in Paris in late 1906 (months after Cheetham's first)

he finds there and takes it home to his astonished wife. Ali's brother visits the cave, is caught by the thieves and (by means of trick-photography) decapitated. In due course, the thieves are eliminated gruesomely at now-wealthy Ali's home by an observant maid.

Edward VII's coronation, postponed until the second Saturday of August 1902, had been covered by nine production companies. On those January evenings, more than six months later, Cheetham offered Rhyl two films of the event, billed as 'Coronation Procession' and 'The King's Procession' respectively. Although the King's illness had kept him from attending the July Coronation troop review at Horse Guards' Parade, he was able to attend the naval one of over a hundred vessels in Spithead, in the Solent, a week after the coronation. It was filmed by fewer companies than the coronation, but Cheetham could choose from, say, Paul's view of ships steaming past the historic *HMS Trafalgar* and 'panoramas' of the fleet by Hepworth, Warwick and Williamson.

Whether in ignorance or by intent, one topical was advertised as 'Boer generals in London'. In fact, it featured the arrival at Southampton of Botha, De la Rey and De Wet in August 1902. They had been generals in the 1899–1902 South African war and leaders of subsequent guerrilla campaigns. They had come to negotiate peace terms with Joseph Chamberlain, Secretary of State for the Colonies. Films of their disembarkation were shot by Gaumont[2] and Paul. Paul's shows them being cheered by a quayside crowd as they negotiate the gangway to be met by Lords Roberts and Kitchener, sensitively wearing civilian clothes. Botha later became Prime Minister of

---

[2] Léon Gaumont and his partners set up *Gaumont et Cie* in 1895. Their UK subsidiary, the Gaumont-British Corporation, was established in 1898 and later became an independent film producer/distributor (Laurent Mannoni in *Who's Who of Victorian Cinema*)

the Transvaal, then first Prime Minister of the Union of South Africa, created in 1910.

Added to the advertised programme 'at the last moment' was 'The Delhi Durbar – shown in all its Oriental splendour'. Although Durbars were traditionally native Indian rulers' assemblies, the December 1902 / January 1903 event was a celebration of Edward VII's accession. Its various components had been covered in 35 films by Warwick, one by Gaumont and two by Paul. The 'grand procession' must surely have best epitomized its 'Oriental splendour'. Some of the 210 participating elephants carried Viceroy Lord Curzon, the Duke of Connaught (representing the King) and their wives as well as members of Indian ruling houses. Other dignitaries rode in landaus. Paul's film, lasting for nearly four minutes, features elephants, landaus, gun-carriages and both marching and mounted soldiers.

'A reproduction of a ten-mile railway ride through the loveliest of Devonshire scenery' suggests the screening of hundreds of feet of phantom-ride film. It could have been compiled from several shorter ones between 50 and 200 feet in length shot in 1899 by Cecil Hepworth from L&SWR locomotives, or in 1898 for Warwick (when he produced his *View from an Engine Front – Ilfracombe*). He relates in his autobiography how he had noticed 'platforms' at the fronts of locomotives 'looking as though they had been made for a camera to be strapped upon'. So he lashed his 1,000ft-capacity camera ('rather like a coffin standing on end') to a convenient safety rail, with a box-like seat for two completing the arrangement.

Two of the three comic films advertised – 'The Greasy Pole' and 'The Punter's Mishap' – featured aquatic pursuits. Several 'greasy pole' films would have been available: Smith's at an 1897 regatta with a pig as the prize, Williamson's and Devant's of 1898, and three produced by Hepworth in 1900 showing dozens of attempts 'over deep water'. Whichever one Cheetham chose, his audiences would have been familiar with its content from enjoying similar contests at Rhyl pier. If 'The Punter's Mishap' was Hepworth's 1900 film of the same name, a boatman would be seen escorting two ladies on a river trip, getting his pole stuck in the mud, edging his way along the punt, falling in and floundering to shore as the vessel (complete with ladies) drifted away. In his *The Immature Punter* of 1898, the unfortunate was left clinging to his pole and struggling in deep water – but at least retaining his hat.

In 'The Nursemaid's Surprise' a tramp steals a bottle from a baby in a pram. Cheetham had several versions to choose from. In Riley's 1898 film of the same name, tramp changes place with infant and is caressed unwittingly by nursemaid. In *The Tramp and the Baby's Bottle* (a joint 1899 effort by Riley Bros and Bamforths of Holmfirth[3]) baby is left unattended while nursemaid walks away with an amorous policeman; tramp appears, snatches a drink but is arrested by policeman when the guilty pair return. Was the late appearance of a friendly dog indented? In Edison's *The Tramp and the Nursing Bottle* of 1901, the vagrant is thrown into a lake by a policeman but is rescued by the occupant of a rowing-boat.

Some early films were hand-coloured frame-by-frame with the aid of a magnifying glass. A 40ft length, lasting less than a minute on screen, could take over a month to complete. Cheetham's patrons might be excused for thinking that all

---

[3] Bamforths started making photographic lantern slides in 1870, specialising in 'life model' narrative sets, with actors posing in front of painted backgrounds. Film production started in 1898, in conjunction with Riley Bros (Richard Brown and John Barnes in *Who's Who of Victorian Cinema*). Bamforths are now better known for their saucy seaside picture-postcards

three comic films were in colour, since their titles were preceded temptingly in his *Journal* advertisement by 'The latest – **Coloured Animated Pictures**'. According to the paper's report, however, just one of them had received this painstaking treatment.

The film advertised as 'Everhart, the great Hoop Manipulator' featured a music-hall performer. Both Warwick and Paul had filmed him in 1902, the latter at Fulham before 14,000 of the King's 'poorer subjects' invited to dinner. Unattributed footage called *Juggler – the Great Everhart* shows him juggling wooden hoops in the air, on his body, along the stage and even up and down his assistant's back.

Also screened was yet another series of fire films. It could have been a repeat of the 'grand finale of fire pictures' of Whit-week 1902, although Edison's *Fire Department of Glasgow, Scotland* ('engines on the way to a fire') had become available, as well as Warwick's brand-new drama entitled *The Great City Fire* (if released early enough in the month). Its firemen are awakened and drive through London streets to a rescue.

By the time Cheetham returned to Rhyl Town Hall for Whit Monday, Tuesday and Wednesday, he had visited over a hundred towns on tour. But he had also been busy with his camera in and around town. While his films of that year's May Day procession and the visit of Col ('Buffalo Bill') Cody are listed in his *Journal* advertisement, 'scenes … in connection with the Rhyl Cycling Club's Outing' must have been shot too late for inclusion. Also on the programme were several repeats: 'The Royal Visit to Rhyl, 1902' ('by request'), 'The Great Delhi Durbar' and *Ali-Baba* (which would be screened again for a whole week before the next annual tour and throughout the 1904 Whit-week). The advertisement made liberal use of bold type and the plural, drawing particular attention to 'The New **Coloured Animated Pictures**, in a set of screamingly comic films' (without actually naming them!). Will Hunter (now billed as 'the singing ventriloquist') and Madame Rose Garton (her songs 'magnificently illustrated with Electric Light' for the first time) provided the live entertainment.

The May Day film was advertised in typical Cheetham fashion: 'come and see yourselves in Animated Photography on the screen – noted people of Rhyl, young men, maidens, children, sweethearts and others – people you all know'. Whatever its original length, several disparate sequences shot from an upstairs window overlooking the Promenade and spliced together comprise the surviving minute-and-a-half. The duly-appointed marshal (a local coach proprietor) leads the procession on horseback, followed by cyclists who have competed in various classes, with the town band close behind. Rhyl Fire Brigade was the sole entry in the 'best and best equipped Fire Brigade turnout (steamer) two or more horses' category. Brigade members ride their appliance, followed by colleagues on a smaller vehicle carrying an extending ladder. The 'neatest and best equipped Fire Brigade turnout (manual) with two or more horses' came from the nearby Bodrhyddan country estate.

The previous year's May Queen rides in a flower-bedecked 'four-in-hand' attended by page and maid, driver resplendent in glistening top hat. Her 1903 successor follows, accompanied by some of her 'court', with the remainder in the next vehicle. The Amalgamated Union of Bakers' prize-winning tableau on its 'lurry' can be identified by tell-tale clouds of smoke and its white-aproned occupants performing tasks of their trade. The L&NWR Company's tableau carries large packing-cases. Tradesmen's entries abound, and among the beasts of burden a diminutive donkey valiantly pulls a sizeable waggon. The camera then focuses on the promenade, where people watch the procession, sit on benches or stroll in a leisurely manner. Bathing machines can be seen on the beach behind them. Towards the end of the surviving footage, several speeding landaus catch up with the rest of the procession. Finally, onlookers enjoy a kerbside performance by the town band.

The one-day visit of Col Cody's American 'Wild West' Show provided Cheetham with his second filming opportunity of the year. The *Record and Advertiser* explains: 'to transport the show to Rhyl requires no less than four special trains and so great will be the tax on the resources of the goods department that day that the delivery of local goods will be entirely suspended for that day'. The performance, staged in a large marquee, included the story of 'the Pioneers of the Plains' who had colonised the American mid-west, told through such re-enactments as 'The Stage Coach "Hold-up"' and 'Attack on the Emigrant Train'. Among the 'Mounted Warriors of the World' portrayed were the United States Cavalry, the Royal English Lancers, Bedouin Arabs and Russian Cossacks.

Cheetham didn't film at the show itself. Rather, he positioned his camera outside the town-centre Lorne Hotel, meeting-place of the fraternal society called the Antediluvian Order of Buffaloes. Although Cody had joined them in the States, he was to be granted honorary membership of the local lodge that day. A deputation met him at the showground in the morning, stayed for the afternoon performance and escorted him in an open carriage to the Lorne. Cheetham's film captures him, complete with 'ten gallon' hat and flowing mane, as he enters the hotel through an expectant crowd. When he reappears, hats are thrown enthusiastically in the air. Finally, two more carriages draw up outside the Lorne for kerbside handshaking before he is driven away. The surviving footage lasts for just over a minute.

Mr Copley of the Nant Hall Hotel in nearby Prestatyn had agreed to become president of Rhyl Cycling Club 'after [it] had been stagnant for a couple of years'. About forty members accepted his invitation to an outing at his premises. Football, rounders and other games were followed by 'a substantial meat tea served al fresco on the lawn'. Then came races and 'a march-past of cyclists for the purpose of enabling Mr Cheetham to take a cinematographic portrait'. He also captured 'a comical spill'. Four male club members appear to have difficulty in separating their cycles lying on the lawn. Three succeed and speed off past the camera. The fourth mounts awkwardly and catches up with one of his fellows so capably that the 'comical spill' must have been specially staged. The surviving 42 seconds feature the 'comical spill' and the *al fresco* meal.

The National Eisteddfod of Wales, with its competitions in such diverse fields as poetry, literature and music, is a major event in the country's cultural calendar. An aura of antiquity is lent by the ceremonies of *Gorsedd y Beirdd* (the Assembly of Bards). Rhyl was to host the Eisteddfod in 1904. So, according to tradition, a proclamation ceremony was held in 1903. Arthur Cheetham shot his fourth and final film of that year in connection with this colourful event. Friday 31 July started with a procession through the town. The *Record and Advertiser* describes it in detail. First came a band playing 'a lively and appropriate selection of Welsh Airs'. Then followed the mayors of Chester, Caernarfon, Bangor, Flint and Beaumaris and the Lord Lieutenant and the High Sheriff of Flintshire. Due prominence was accorded to the *Gorsedd*, all in their flowing robes and preceded by a carriage conveying Archdruid *Hwfa Môn* (aka Congregational minister the Reverend Rowland Williams) resplendent in gold breastplate and crown with oak-leaf and acorn motifs. Members were followed by uniformed officials carrying the ceremonial sword and the symbolic *Corn Hirlas* (horn of plenty).

The proclamation ceremony was held in a purpose-built stone circle on the sand-dunes. The scene, reported the *Record and Advertiser*, was 'one mass of people ... the majority of whom were evidently English visitors, on whom the ceremony, though unintelligible, appeared to exercise considerable fascination'. After the *Gorsedd* prayer had been intoned, the ceremonial sword was thrice unsheathed and re-sheathed. Each time, 'in a voice which even the high wind could not silence', the Archdruid asked *A oes heddwch?* (Is there peace?). At first, it was only those in the circle who answered *Heddwch*. But by the third time of asking, the assembled multitude responded 'with a most curious but grand effect'. Among other elements of the ceremony was the initiation of new *Gorsedd* members. The procession then wended its way back through town. Finally, the local Executive Committee entertained guests to luncheon.

Whatever Cheetham's camera captured that day, the film has not survived, and the local newspapers provide no details. It was screened throughout the week commencing Monday 28 September as part of 'a huge new programme as arranged for the principal cities and towns of England'. The venue was described as being 'on the Victoria Pier', whether the Bijou or the temporary building erected on the site of the former Grand Pavilion, which had been destroyed by fire in 1901.

Also screened that week were 'A Trip to Norway', 'The British Navy (in a new and fine series of pictures)', *Ali-Baba*, *Nature's Unseen World* and repeats of recent Cheetham films. *Nature's Unseen World* was a science series produced by the newly-established Charles Urban Trading Company.[4] In *Cheese Mites*, for example, a man eating bread and cheese uses his reading glass to read his newspaper and then to examine his cheese. To his horror, it is alive with mites (actually filmed through a microscope). So he leaves in disgust.

Material for 'A Trip to Norway' could have been provided by Hepworth's recent five-part *Norway* series or Paul's longer *Norway Revisited with the Animatograph* (the name of a ciné camera he had designed). One of Hepworth's films, *Norway – Hardanger and Geiranger Fjords*, had been taken from a boat passing cliffs, houses, a church and a waterfall. As to the 'new and fine series of pictures': 'new' may indicate more films of the 1902 Spithead review. Madame Garton and Will Hunter were joined by Jimmy Charters of Merrie Men fame (billed this time as a comedian, rather than a dancer) and boy pianist Gus Cheetham in this send-off for the forthcoming tour.

Films mentioned in this chapter which can be viewed on *YouTube*: *Ali-Baba et les quarante voleurs 1905* (Pathé), *Coronation of Edward VII* (unused/unissued material uploaded by British Pathé), *The Delhi Durbar Robert W. Paul, 1903*

---

[4] Charles Urban had been manager of the Warwick Trading Company. Before arriving in England to be head of their predecessors Maguire and Baucus, he had been in charge of a Detroit kinetoscope parlor (Luke McKernan in *Who's Who of Victorian Cinema*)

(Paul), *View from an Engine Front – Ilfracombe* (Hepworth for Warwick), *The Tramp and the Baby's Bottle* (Riley/Bamforth but entitled *Woman, baby, policeman and tramp gags in 1900*) and *Juggler – the Great Everhart* (unattributed)

On '*Britain on Film*' *BFI Player*: *Rhyl May Day Procession 1903; Buffalo Bill's Visit to Rhyl; Rhyl Cycling Club Outing to Nant Hall, Prestatyn* (all by Cheetham) and *Cheese Mites 1903* (Urban, but ending before the man's expression of horror)

On *BFI Screenonline 1900s Films: Norway – Hardanger and Geiranger Fjords* (Hepworth)

On '*Britain on Film*' *BFI Player*, but not mentioned in the chapter: *Conway Castle – Panoramic View on the L.&N.W. Railway 1898* (the American Mutoscope & Biograph Company). An example of a hand-coloured film

Chapter 10

1904 and 1905: 'Slate Quarrying' and 'Beautiful Wales'

Films about north-west Wales figured large in Cheetham's 1904 and 1905 fare at Rhyl Town Hall. Top of the bill in his advertisements for Whit-week 1904 was his own 'Unique set of Silvograph Copyright Pictures (only just taken) of Slate Quarrying in North Wales showing the hazardous work of slate getting, slate breaking, splitting, dressing, gathering refuse, the use of the ariel [sic] railway'.[1] 'This industry', observed the *Record and Advertiser*, 'is absolutely unknown to people from the English counties, and in fact in many parts of Wales, where the people have little opportunity of getting to the quarries'.

Also advertised were 'The Far East War', 'Desperate Affray with Poachers', 'new [un-named] comic pictures' and films Cheetham had taken at unspecified locations in Rhyl during the previous week. 'Trip to Norway', 'The British Navy' and *Ali Baba* were screened again. And, rather than engaging guest performers, he relied entirely on Madame Rose Garton's 'new illustrated songs' and son Gus at the piano for live entertainment.

The subject of 'The Far East War' was that between Russia and Japan. The *Record and Advertiser* had reported in February on the initial Japanese attack on Russian-held Port Arthur in Manchuria, and several films on the conflict were available.

---

[1] 'Ariel railway' must surely mean 'aerial ropeway': the cables extending across open-pit slate quarries with waggons suspended from them and raised or lowered to reach the various working levels. They were called 'Blondins' locally, after the noted 19th century tightrope walker Charles Blondin. Cheetham's mention of this feature suggests that he had filmed at the open-pit quarries at Bethesda, Llanberis or the Nantlle Valley

Warwick and Urban had sent camera-men to cover the Japanese and Russian sides respectively, producing topicals such as *Japanese Reservists Leaving for the Front* and a series entitled *With the Russian Army in Siberia*. Among the dramatic reconstructions Cheetham could choose from were Paul's *An Affair of Outposts*, in which Japanese ambush Russians, and his *All for the Love of a Geisha* (she is kidnapped by the Russians but is rescued by Japanese soldiers and an English naval officer). Russian efforts are foiled in the Sheffield Photo Company's *A Dash with the Despatch* and *Russians ambush a Japanese Convoy*. In the former, a Japanese despatch rider escapes from a Cossack ambush, and in the latter his compatriots turn the tables on their attackers.[2]

'Desperate Affray with Poachers' was the title Cheetham gave to William Haggar's 3-minute drama *A Desperate Poaching Affray*, perhaps to avoid identifying with the 'baddies'. They are chased by gamekeepers, policemen and dogs. Pursued and pursuers alike make liberal use of fisticuffs and firearms, and a final mid-stream struggle ends in arrest.[3]

January 1905 saw a major change in the organisation of what was to be Cheetham's final annual tour. He purchased a 16-hp motor-car locally to undertake trips of a few days at a time, enabling him to return home frequently to attend to other

---

[2] The Sheffield Photo Company was established as a photographic business in 1900 by Frank Mottershaw. Productive between 1903 and 1909, their most celebrated films were produced after his eldest son returned from a year working for R.W. Paul (booklet accompanying the BFI's *Early Cinema, Primitives and Pioneers* DVD, p. 9 and *IMDb* [International Media Database]: *Mottershaw filmography*)

[3] Essex-born William Haggar would tour the fairgrounds of south Wales and south-west England with his portable cinema, fronted by ornate façade and mechanical organ. The films he produced between 1901 and 1914 included over 50 dramas and comedies, acted mainly by family members (Peter Yorke. *William Haggar (1851–1925) fairground film-maker*)

business. It carried passengers and equipment, as well as compressed gas (presumably for places lacking an electricity supply). Rail detours, changing trains and then travelling by road from stations to venues up to three miles away would thus be avoided. 'In this way', emphasises the copy submitted to both local papers in April, 'many places can be visited where under ordinary circumstances the expense of awkward journeys and the conveyance of luggage would make the place prohibitive.'

However, according to grandson Stanley Cheetham, when interviewed in 1998: 'the route was always chosen to follow a railway line because cars were so unreliable, and if they were stuck they would get on the train'. On one occasion, his father Gustavus had told him, the car broke down at the top of a hill. So 'they coasted down … to a farm gate and persuaded the farmer to lend them a horse to tow [the car] into the nearest town [to be repaired] and continue the journey'. Trips to Gloucestershire, Oxfordshire, Staffordshire, Leicestershire, Shropshire, Cheshire, and Flintshire totalling 1,500 miles had already been made.

'Handsome in appearance, upholstered in red leather and most comfortable in every way', the 'Silvograph' motor-car (what else could it be called?) was also available for trips in and around Rhyl in the summer. In 1908 a brand-new Darracq (shades of *Genevieve*!) replaced the original vehicle. An advertisement in that year's programme-booklet for the Central Hall cinema offered 'Motor Tours in Beautiful Wales … for hire by the day, half-day or trip'.

Cheetham's first Town Hall appearances in 1905 were on Easter Monday and Tuesday. Among the films advertised under the heading 'A Tour in Beautiful Wales' was 'The

Blaenau Festiniog Underground Quarries'. Hepworth's *The Story of a piece of Slate* ('from quarry to builder's yard') and Warwick's *Through a Slate Quarry in North Wales* had been released since his own 'Unique set of Silvograph Copyright Pictures'. Underground quarries (as in Blaenau Ffestiniog) would not employ the 'ariel railway' he had filmed then, so he may have acquired one of them – perhaps in grudging acknowledgment of its superiority.

'A Tour in Beautiful Wales' also included a selection of railway films. Hepworth's *A Phantom Ride on the Cambrian Coast* (on a standard-gauge train) ended after about five minutes below the towering rock of Harlech Castle. 'A Trip on the Festiniog Narrow Guage [sic] Railway' featured the Blaenau Ffestiniog / Porthmadog line. It was soon to be advertised in the *Cambrian News* as 'the far-famed Festiniog (or Toy) Railway, from which [tourists] will see the most enchanting scenery in North Wales'. So 'A Trip ...' may have been *A Ride on a Toy Railway*, also by Hepworth.

Finally, 'The Ascent of Snowdon' was Warwick's *To Snowdon's Summit on a Motor Car*, featuring Dunlop Rubber Company director and future MP Harvey du Cros and Canadian poet Charles Sangster. In May 1904, following an unsuccessful January attempt, they drove an Ariel to the summit along the mountain railway's narrow-gauge railway track in a single day. But it is not clear which part of the endeavour figured in this two-minute film. du Cros and Sangster were not, however, the first to drive up Snowdon. Charles Jarrott and W.M. Letts, partners in a car-importing company, had preceded them by 12 days. They took just 61 minutes, but did not go all the way to the summit.

Pride of place in Cheetham's newspaper advertisements was, however, accorded not to 'A Tour in Beautiful Wales' but to several dramatic films. Pathé's hand-coloured 15-minute *La Belle au bois dormant / The Sleeping Beauty* acts out the well-known story of the princess who pricks her finger on a spinning-wheel, falls asleep and is awakened by the prince who wins her hand in marriage. The wife-and-mother in Mitchell & Kenyon's *Tragic Elopement* forsakes her family for a lover. Husband pursues their getaway car on a motor-bike, but remorseful wife sacrifices herself by saving him from lover's bullet. The eponymous criminal in Gaumont's *The Pickpocket* relieves a 'toff' of his watch, knocks him down and flees. But in spite of commandeering a bicycle and employing various other tactics, he is caught by the police.

'The North Sea Outrage' recalled an incident of October 1904 when Russia's Baltic Fleet was on its way to the Pacific to reinforce her Far East Fleet in the war against Japan. Hull trawlers fishing on the Dogger Bank were mistaken for Japanese torpedo-boats. The Russians opened fire, sinking one trawler, damaging others and causing injury and death. Cheetham had a choice of films of damaged trawlers in port shot by Warwick and Hepworth to illustrate this event.

However, his advertisements unaccountably refer to 'A Tragedy in the Air – The North Sea Outrage', as if the hapless trawlermen had been attacked from Russian military balloons! But the *Record and Advertiser*'s news columns clearly recognise two separate films: 'The North Sea Outrage' **and** 'A Tragedy in the Air'. So the 'Tragedy' may have been that experienced by the balloonists in Pathé's part-acted, part-animated 2½-minute *Un drame dans les aires / A drama in the air*. They suffer a lightning strike but are saved by a boatman when their gondola falls into the sea.

Three of the seven 'new comics' advertised can be readily identified. Two were by Hepworth: while the navvies in *Don't Interfere with a Coalheaver* manhandle an inquisitive sightseer in a white suit with predictable results, the unfortunate soldier in *His Superior Officer* (patriotically advertised by Cheetham as 'Tommy Atkins and his Superior Officer') loses his girlfriend not to one but to three of higher rank.

'Two Old Maids' appears to be G.A. Smith's *Scandal Over the Teacup* of 1900. Smith's wife and a man in 'drag' chatter incessantly for nearly a minute and a half, expressing surprise and casting secretive glances rearwards. One can imagine the occasional 'Never!' or 'You don't say!'.

While 'Fun with Cobbler's Wax', 'The Man with the Painted Jacket', 'The Hungry Traveller' and 'The Tantalising Dinner' may be titles of Cheetham's making, the latter must surely portray an eventful meal, such as in Méliès's *Le Répas Fantastique / A Fantastical Meal*, the Lumière film of the same name and American producer Siegmund Lubin's *Eating Dinner Under Difficulties*.[4] Méliès and Lubin both employ trick-photography to subject their respective diners to a succession of mishaps with elusive furniture, while the former introduces further chaos. The sight of a dish dropped by a clumsy waitress in the Lumières' *Le Répas Fantastique* does not bode well for their diner. Then follows more cinematic trickery. But this 1905 film may not have been available in time for screening by Cheetham at Easter.

His second 1905 Town Hall booking was for the Monday, Tuesday and Wednesday of Whit-week. Top of the bill was 'Whirling the Worlds, Or a Trip to the Sun'. Although

---

[4] Siegmund Lubin's Philadelphia-based company started producing films in 1897. He was a major figure in the US film industry up to the outbreak of World War I and had a chain of nearly 100 cinemas on the east coast by 1918 (Deac Rossell in *Who's Who of Victorian Cinema*)

advertised as 'the Rage of the present London Season', it might well have been described as lasting for some 20 minutes (about five times the average duration of films at that time). This Méliès sci-fi production, entitled *Le Voyage à Travers L'Impossible / The Impossible Voyage*, employs a range of trick-photography. Towards the end, for example, a train including a refrigerated truck and a submarine takes off from a mountain-top. Buoyed up by balloons, it traverses space, only to be swallowed by the sun and crash-land in its interior. One traveller protects his fellows by bundling them into the truck. But on opening the door, he finds them frozen stiff. So he lights a fire to thaw them out, and they all return to earth in the submarine.

An audacious tramp, an expectant soldier, an inebriated burglar, a would-be lover and a gate-crashing railway passenger are among the characters featured in the comedies advertised. One of the rogues in Warwick's *Tramps in Clover* poses as a policeman to steal beef from a butcher. The flirt in Gaumont's *The Amorous Militiaman* suffers the ignominy of being scrubbed by a washerwoman. The intruder in *The Burglar and the Girls*, produced by the Clarendon Film Company, ties a girl up and gets drunk, only to be ejected by her sisters.[5] The gigolo in Gaumont's *The Masher's Dilemma* is suggestively handed a baby by a flower-seller as he rings a girl's doorbell ('masher' can mean 'a man who attempts to force his attentions on a woman'). And the intruder in Pathé's *Voyageur peu gêné / The Cheeky Traveller* takes over a railway compartment with his luggage, puts the light out and gets ready to sleep – much to the chagrin of the other occupant, who ejects him and returns to

---

[5] The Clarendon Film Company's name was derived from their original premises off Croydon's Clarendon Road. Founded in 1904, they initially dealt with ciné cameras. Co-founder Percy Stow had previously been associated with Cecil Hepworth. Clarendon produced many comedies, distributed by Gaumont, and grew to be a major pre-WW1 film producer (*Wikipedia* and on-line *Movie Movie*)

his corner (and his newspaper) in peace.

On the other hand, the innocent creatures in Edison's *Elephants Shooting the Chutes at Luna Park* (on New York's Coney Island) are an unwitting source of amusement as they descend the steep incline, splash down and enjoy a cool bath before being coaxed back to *terra firma* by their keepers.

The title 'Soap Bubbles' suggests children having fun, as in Edison's *Making Soap Bubbles* of 1897 ('gathered about a tub of soap suds, pushing and jostling [and] blowing soap bubbles from clay pipes') and Pathé's *Les Bulles de savon / Blowing Bubbles* of 1904. The latter was marketed as a '*scène comique*' and described obligingly in English as 'a very pretty natural scene of children blowing soap bubbles'.

Unaccountably embedded in the list of comic films is the Sheffield Photo Company's five-minute drama *The Coiners*, in which counterfeiters are raided by the police. Their car blows up in the ensuing chase. And, just like 'Fun with Cobbler's Wax' etc at Easter, 'My Pal Curly' may have been a film to which Cheetham gave his own title.

While the apparent absence of live performers at Easter 1905 might be explained by the lengthy list of films advertised, the 20-odd minutes of 'Whirling the Worlds, Or a Trip to the Sun' do not seem to have precluded Madame Garton's participation in the 'full two-hours' of her husband's Whit-week shows.

Films mentioned in this chapter which can be viewed on *YouTube*: *Desperate Poaching Affray* (Haggar), *Un drame dans les aires / A drama in the air* (Pathé), *Le Répas Fantastique / A Fantastical Meal* (Méliès), *Le repas fantastique* (Lumière: no. 2007, 29 minutes into *Films Lumière 12*, a 40-minute on-line collection of films, not numbered consecutively) and *Le Voyage à travers L'impossible / The Impossible Voyage* (Méliès)

On *BFI Screenonline 1900s Films: Scandal Over the Teacups* (Smith)

On *YouTube,* but not mentioned in the chapter: *Slate Railway in North Wales, 1930's – Film 8537* (Huntley film Archives). A 13-minute film mainly about the 'Blondins' and the internal narrow-gauge railway system at the Dinorwic quarry in Llanberis

Also on *YouTube,* but not mentioned in the chapter: *Ffestiniog Railway 150th Anniversary – The Gravity Slate Train.* Several films on *YouTube* show modern passenger trains on this popular tourist line, but this one re-creates the engine-less method of transporting slate down from the quarries at Blaenau Ffestiniog to the quay at Porthmadog

Chapter 11

Cinema Proprietor

Arthur Cheetham joined the ranks of early cinema proprietors in 1906 when he opened his Central Hall in Rhyl's Market Street, although he continued to produce films occasionally until 1912. Defining a cinema as a fixed venue dedicated to regular motion picture entertainment, Luke McKernan identifies the Daily Bioscope in Bishopsgate Street as almost certainly London's first, accommodating 120 patrons. It opened on 23 May 1906 – three days before Cheetham's Central Hall. Others followed the Daily Bioscope in the capital later that year.[1] Some time in the same year, the upper floor of the Sefton Park Assembly Rooms in Aigburth, Liverpool became the Aigburth Assembly Picturedrome, with seating for 300 on long wooden benches.[2] Notably, observing that 'a theatre devoted entirely to the display of living pictures is a new thing in this country', the *Kinematograph Weekly* reported that the Balham Empire music-hall had opened its doors as such in the summer of 1907. The programme, 'exclusively provided by the celebrated firm of Pathe Freres', lasted for about two hours.[3]

Cheetham's second cinema was in Aberystwyth. He had first visited the town on tour in January 1897, when the *Aberystwyth Observer* reported on the 'living pictures [and] a number of other photographic views' screened at the

---

[1] Luke McKernan. 'Diverting Time: London Cinemas and their Audiences, 1906–1914' in *The London Journal*, July 2007 (on-line)

[2] *Cinema Treasures. Rivoli Cinema, Liverpool* (on-line)

[3] *Kinematograph Weekly*, August 29, 1907, p. 254

Assembly Rooms. But in September 1910 he took over the New Market Hall, which had been hosting concerts, dances etc since late 1897. Its first night as a cinema was held under the patronage of the Mayor and Corporation. Within weeks, about 300 new seats had been installed (with tip-up ones in the 'best' section), thereby gaining the *Cambrian News*'s seal of approval as 'an acquisition to the town in the long winter evenings'. Advertisements placed in the paper in early 1913 emphasised that it was 'the first and only entertainment in Aberystwyth ever to run all the year round'.

Colwyn Bay's Public Hall had also been among the venues visited by Cheetham in 1897. He returned with his 'Silvograph Pictures, three times daily' for a few weeks between September 1908 and January 1909. But Friday, 22 December 1911 saw him opening the town's first permanent cinema, on the site of a former mews and an earlier chapel. The handbill he printed for the occasion proudly announced that the proceeds and retiring collection at the matinee would be donated to Colwyn Bay Cottage Hospital and those at the two evening shows to the town's advertising association.[4]

The cinema had been designed by local architect S. Colwyn Foulkes, responsible for *art deco* ones at Rhyl, Flint and Bebington in the 1930s. He won the 1936 'Cinema of the Year' award for his Palace Cinema in Conwy, adjudged to be sensitively in tune with its surroundings in the historic town. It has been granted Grade II status by *Cadw* (the body responsible for Welsh historic monuments) and still retains its exterior castle-like appearance.[5]

The booklet which Cheetham also printed for the opening of his Colwyn Bay cinema congratulates Colwyn Foulkes on

[4] Colwyn Bay cinema handbill: National Library of Wales
[5] *Cinema Treasures. Palace Cinema, High Street, Conwy* (on-line, including interior and exterior photographs)

'the admirable manner in which he has overcome the difficulties attending the adaptation of the premises to their new purpose'. The foyer's domed ceiling was 'exquisitely modelled in plaster' and its floor paved with 'Roman Glass Mosaic of rich and beautiful colours'. Its walls were of Indian teak 'in character with the shops on either side'. The shops are still there, as well as two new ones on the site of the foyer, but it is difficult to imagine how they could have enhanced the cinema's external appearance. The booklet also claims that the illuminated sign in the form of the prow of a Viking ship projecting from the façade demonstrated that 'even an illuminated sign may be a thing of beauty'. *Chaque un à son goût* (or, as we say in Welsh: *Pawb at y peth y bo*).

Safety was ensured by placing the 'Operating [projection] Chamber' outside the building, so that there was 'no communication ... except the openings through which the picture is projected on to the screen [and which] if necessary, can be closed instantaneously by means of an iron shutter'.[6] Keeping audience and projector apart was an acknowledgement of the danger of fire when ciné film was made from unstable, highly flammable nitro-cellulose. A film might ignite if exposed to excessive heat in the projector. Several conflagrations occurred, causing death by flames, smoke or the resulting rush to escape. In 1907, under the headline 'Pictures on Fire', the *Rhyl Record and Advertiser* reported that 'during a display of living pictures at the Central Hall, Market Street, a rod [surely 'reel'] of film caught fire'. But fortunately, it was removed from the building immediately without causing damage. The Colwyn Bay cinema's 'Operating Chamber' still stands, as a reminder of the building's former use. The town's Public Hall screens films occasionally.

---

[6] *Opening of the Colwyn Bay Cinema in connection with Arthur Cheetham's Picture Theatres.* [1911], pp. [3]-[4]: National Library of Wales

In December 1912, from his recently-acquired Bijou Cinema on Manchester's Cheetham Hill Road, where he had 'every facility for seeing all the latest productions', Cheetham launched a twice-weekly series of 'special programmes' for all his venues. Each one was to include a long 'star' feature. The first (according to the copy submitted to the *Rhyl Journal*) was a 'western' entitled *The Trapper's Bride*, which lasted for over half an hour. The three-storey 1903 building on the Cheetham Hill Road site is occupied by a group of fashion businesses, but the cinema's auditorium stands at the rear. Incidentally, when interviewed in 1977 Mrs Gwen Cordery emphasised her father's insistence on being called 'Cheetham', the pronunciation of the 'th' as 't' apparently having connotations of fraudulent trading! One wonders whether his preference was respected by the residents of Cheetham [pronounced 'Cheetam'] Hill Road!

In early 1914 Cheetham was granted the licence of the Bijou cinema in Eccles, near Manchester. He promptly advertised its fare in the *Eccles Journal* as 'the finest pictures in Lancashire' and offered children under 12 years of age half-price entry to the first house every evening and to the Monday and Saturday matinees. He also drew attention to his Cheetham Hill Road, Rhyl, Colwyn Bay and Aberystwyth connections. The paper reported that *Father* (the first film he screened in Eccles) contained 'the finest fire scene ever put on screen at that time'. It also commented favourably on 'the clearness and absolute steadiness of the pictures', attributing them to 'the proprietor's long experience and perfect knowledge of the animated picture business'. However long Cheetham occupied the Bijou, its last known record dates from 1915.[7]

---

[7] Tony Flynn. *The History of Eccles Cinemas and Theatres*, 1986, p. 2

Arthur Cheetham's Rhyl Town Hall swansong had occurred several months before the opening of his Central Hall cinema. For three nights in late February 1906 he hired the venue for a programme of interest, topical, comic and dramatic films. Then, finding the Friday and Saturday to be free, he ended his long association with it with two extra performances.

Top of the bill was 'British Industries: Sausage-Making', shot at the Palethorpes factory in Dudley Port and tracing production from farm to customer. Dealing also with pork pies, it appears to have lasted for some three-quarters of an hour, since it was advertised as being 'about half-a-mile long'. Local Palethorpes representative Richard Sykes had been instrumental in securing it, and he augmented Madam Garton's contributions with gramophone records in the intervals. Obliging with piano solos was not Gus Cheetham but his younger brother, 13-year-old Bernard. Their father's 1902 royal visit film was (as the *Journal* respectfully put it) screened 'in a manner that recalled that great occasion to the minds of all who saw it'.

Three of the four comic films on the programme were by Clarendon. The two rascals in their *Willie and Tim in the Motor Car* find that a chauffeur has left his charge unattended outside the gates of a country house. So they steal it and go for a spin with their girlfriends. Chauffeur returns and gives chase on a motor-bike aided by the police, who arrest the pair when they get stuck in a lake. Willie and Tim first appeared in 1896 as comic-strip characters in the weekly *Illustrated Chips* as the tramps Weary Willie and Tired Tim. They also featured in other comic films, such as Haggar's *Weary Willie and Tired Tim – the Gunpowder Plot*, when they stick a poker in a barrel misleadingly labelled 'Beer' – with obvious consequences. In *The Stolen Pig*, Cheetham's audiences would have seen an old woman stuffing the animal in question into a sack, then a butcher replacing it with his son. And the setting for *When father got a holiday* is a large family's cycle ride.

In Hepworth's comedy *The Traveller Bewitched*, trick-photography ensures the disappearance of the main character's hotel breakfast table (twice), two buses (together with the horses and passengers of one of them), two trains, himself and finally his bag – in a puff of smoke. No wonder that one of this film's other titles was *The Jonah Man*!

Also screened that week were *The Ship on Fire* and Clarendon's *The Sailor's Wedding*. Whoever produced the former, the *Journal*'s description of it as 'exciting' when screened at Rhyl by New Century Pictures later in the year suggests that these two films had something in common: the bridegroom-to-be in the latter escapes from a burning vessel in time to save his fiancée from a villain's clutches.

Chapter 12

1906: Rhyl Central Hall's First Year

Arthur Cheetham opened his Central Hall cinema on Saturday 26 May 1906, a week before the Whit week-end. The main attraction for that evening and the following week was Edison's 11½–minute *The Train Wreckers*. Its young heroine is knocked unconscious by villains intent on de-railing trains. They leave her lying on the track. But she is rescued by her engine-driver fiancé perched precariously on his locomotive's cowcatcher, and the would-be wreckers are eliminated in the ensuing shoot-out.

Gifts had been offered to the first 150 patrons buying tickets for the opening night, during which Cheetham informed his audience that the single 8.30 pm 'house' would be augmented by a 7 o'clock one from Whit-Monday, with afternoon matinees on wet days and bank holidays. A fixed screen and an electrically-driven projector separated from the audience had, he explained, been installed as features not considered feasible for 'an exhibition fitted for a few days only'.

Although his weekly advertisements in the *Journal* and the *Record and Advertiser* had initially announced that 'the Silvograph Electric Animated Pictures ... with change of pictures every week' were to close in September, performances continued to the end of the year – and into 1907 and beyond. Rather than listing films in the advertisements, he relied on the news columns for publicity. This coverage, albeit incomplete, indicates a diet of drama and comedy in the main. While some American and French films are mentioned, frequent reference to the work of companies such as Hepworth and Warwick suggests a preponderance of English material.

Queen Victoria's grand-daughter Princess Victoria Eugenie was to marry Spanish King Alfonzo XIII in Madrid on the Thursday before Whitsun. So Cheetham arranged for his London agent to acquire a film of the event and post it to him in time for the Bank Holiday Monday matinee. Taken for Pathé by Spanish director Segundo de Chomón, it showed the newly-weds leaving the church watched by the Prince and Princess of Wales and other royals. Afterwards, when the wedding procession was on its way back to the royal palace, an assassin threw a bomb from an upstairs window, causing injury and death. But Alfonzo and Victoria Eugenie were unharmed.

Also on the Whit-week bill was another Edison drama: the 10½-minute *The Great Train Robbery*. Its 'baddies' blow up a locked chest on a train and remove mail-bags from it, hurl the fireman to the track and relieve the passengers of their valuables. They then order the driver to proceed to a pre-arranged point, where they retrieve their horses and gallop off. But a local posse is raised, and the thieves are killed in the final show-down.

The two 'westerns' screened that year were produced not in the USA, but in France and England respectively. While the abducted stage-coach passengers in Pathé's *Indiens et cow-boys* are saved by *les cow-boys*, the heroine of Hepworth's *The Squatter's Daughter* is released by her father before her captors can burn her at the stake.

A knowledge of American slang would have helped Central Hall audiences understand that Edison's 11-minute *Rounding up of the "Yeggmen"* was about bank robbers adept at blowing up safes. Carrying their haul in a sack and firing as they go, they flee pursuing locals through woodland, across a river by boat and then on horseback to a waiting railway engine, only to be involved in a head-on collision!

Romance and sentimentality featured in the Central Hall's dramatic fare. The heroine of *Held to Ransom*, produced by the Alpha Trading Company of St Albans, has been kidnapped by blackmailers, so she sends carrier pigeons to summon her fiancé.[1] Warwick's *Me and my Two Pals* and the Sheffield Photo Company's *Lost in the Snow* both feature a faithful dog – trailing a man who has stolen its young owner's cat in the former and leading distraught parents through the elements to be reunited with their child in the latter. The 'copy' submitted to the *Journal* for the Gaumont film variously called *The Runaway Match, Marriage by Motor* and *Elopement à la Mode* re-named it unaccountably as *A marriage in a motor car*, even adding the 'spoiler' 'Love conquers all'. This film's determined couple reach the church before the bride's irate father can prevent their marriage. His car breaks down on the way, but he is eventually reconciled to their union.

A survey of the comic films screened that year reveals a plethora of characters either deserving of the fate meted out to them or entirely blameless. For example: marital infidelity abounds in Alpha's *Why the Typist got the Sack* and Williamson's *A Day on his Own*. Suspicious wife follows errant husband and secretary to a café in the former, while husband is discovered at a fun-fair with **two** female companions in the

---

[1] The Alpha Trading Company was set up in 1904 by Arthur Melbourne-Cooper, co-directing films with R.W. Paul until 1909 but continuing independently up to 1914. (*IMDb. Biography, Arthur Melbourne Cooper* by Martin Ayres). Melbourne-Cooper specialised in films featuring animated models, such as *A Dream of Toyland* (1907), in which dolls come to life in a boy's dream. It can be viewed on the East Anglian Film Archive's website

latter. And the tramps who attack a lady cyclist in Warwick's *Catching a Tartar* are unaware that she is an accomplished boxer. The consequences need no explanation.

Among the innocent victims of filmic fun were men of the cloth, a novice cyclist and a householder who suffers a break-in. While the cleric in Hepworth's *The Annual Trip of the Mothers' Meeting* has trouble escorting his charges on a day-trip to the seaside, his counterpart in Clarendon's *Convict and Curate* is forced to exchange clothes with a fleeing jail-bird. If 'Auntie's First Cycle Lesson' was Gaumont's *Auntie's Cycling Lesson*, the hapless lady would be seen colliding with a policeman and several other people. But if Paul's *Auntie's First Attempt at Cycling*, she is showered by boxes dropping off a van. Insult is added to injury in Pathé's *Les Dévaliseurs noctunes / Burglars at work*: the villains escape on the very bicycle the hapless householder has used to summon the *Gendarmerie*.

The Lost Child is an unlikely title for a comedy. Two US producers, the American Mutoscope & Biograph Company and Siegmund Lubin, issued separate versions in late 1905. But Lubin soon re-named his film *The Kidnapped Child*. So Cheetham is likely to have screened Mutoscope & Biograph's 9-minute production (they were by then filming at 35mm). In it, a mother observes a stranger placing something in a basket and accuses him of kidnapping her child. She chases him, followed by her cook, her washerwoman, a policeman, a nursemaid with a baby-carriage, an old man in an invalid-chair, two girls, a farmer and his family, a *dago* pushing a junk-cart and a one-legged boy on crutches. Cornered, the suspect opens his basket to reveal nothing but a guinea pig, and the 'lost' child is found snoozing in the dog's kennel.[2]

---

[2] Charles Musser. *Before the Nickelodeon. Edwin S. Porter and the Edison Manufacturing Company*, p. 394 (for the two versions of *The Lost Child*) and *AFI* [the American Film Institute] *Catalog of Feature Films* (for the plot of the Mutoscope & Biograph version)

The *Journal* mentions 'A Drama in Mid Air' alongside 'highly entertaining numbers' such as *The Traveller Bewitched* (again). So it appears to be not Pathé's *Un drame dans les aires / A drama in the air* (about the balloon which suffers a lightning strike) but Alpha's nine-minute comedy *Rescued in Mid Air*. Its eccentric inventor rescues an airborne lady in his fantastic flying machine when her parasol-aided descent is intercepted by a church spire. Photographic trickery features large in *Rescued in Mid Air*, as in other comic films screened at the Central Hall that year. The drunkard in Warwick's *How Jones saw the Derby* views the famous race run backwards. And G.A. Smith's *Grandma's Reading Glass* employs a circular cut-out mask to mimic close-ups of several objects as if being examined by her grandson through a magnifying glass.

Although now proprietor of a permanent cinema screening films of up to 20 minutes duration and more, Cheetham did not appear to have disregarded shorter ones featuring traditional music-hall 'turns'. The title of Warwick's *The Mysterious Bag* puts one in mind of Julie Andrews extracting impossibly large objects from her carpet-bag in *Mary Poppins*. The 'beautifully coloured "Quick Change Artist" ' may have been Warwick's 1902 film of a performer called Armandus, who coincidentally had presented his 'marvellous changes [and] impersonations of celebrities of all nations' on stage in Rhyl that year. And if the title 'The French Illusionist' is indicative of the country of origin, possible contenders would be Pathé's *L'Illusionniste mondain* of 1901 and their *L'Illusionniste* of 1897. Both, unsurprisingly, portray a disappearing act.

Cheetham seems to have been quite happy to screen pantomime films at the 'wrong' time of the year, viz *Ali Baba* in the January, Whit-week and September of 1903, then again in Whit-week 1904 – not to mention *Sleeping Beauty* at Easter 1905. So it is not surprising to find him presenting *Robinson Crusoe, Puss in Boots* and *Sleeping Beauty* at the Central Hall during three successive weeks in July 1906!

Among the interest films shown that year were Warwick's brand-new *Whaling off the Shetlands,* their earlier *Head Dresses of various nations* and Urban's recent *Wonders of the Deep.* Described in the *Journal* as 'an interesting object lesson to adults and children alike', *Whaling* gratuitously featured 'all the phases of the capture and cutting up of a 70 ton whale'. *Head Dresses* ('a most charming coloured picture … interesting alike to males as well as to females') was promptly re-named 'Head Dresses of **all** nations' by Cheetham. Also coloured, *Wonders of the Deep* was a 'most artistic and wonderful' 25-minute compilation from an earlier series called *Wonders of the World.* As to the topicals: some of Cheetham's earlier efforts were given a new lease of life, among them being his two May Day films, *Blackburn Rovers v West Bromwich Albion, E.H. Williams's Merrie Men,* children on Rhyl beach, the Cycling Club outing and the enigmatic Rhyl/Wrexham football match.

Music had played a part in Cheetham's film-shows since March 1897, when T. Amos Jones and Mme Marie Williamson entertained his Town Hall audience. But it was to assume increased importance during his first year at the Central Hall. One *Journal* report refers to 'illustrated songs introduced at intervals'. But in mid-August, at the height of the season (when three 'houses' were being offered and the extra wet-day shows moved to 11 am) the *Record and Advertiser* exhorted readers to be 'early on Monday, as this is the day when [records of] Madame Patti's songs are given'. Then, on one September afternoon, an 'invitation gramophone concert' of operatic arias, a Gregorian chant and solos by Melba, Patti, Caruso, Dan Leno etc was held. A similar event on the following Wednesday was reported as being attended by 'some of the elite of the town'. It seems to have been a success, since a weekly series began in early October (when the afternoon 'houses' had been discontinued). Both local newspapers reported on some of them in detail. Bands and orchestral items are mentioned. Also grand opera, Gilbert & Sullivan and soloists such as Caruso, Patti and Melba, not to mention Harry Lauder and George Grossmith. Drama was represented by the famous actor/manager H. Beerbohm Tree reciting Falstaff's speech on 'Honour' from Shakespeare's *Henry V, Part I.*

The gramophone concert season culminated in late November with Handel's *Messiah*, which was repeated in early December 'in response to many requests'. Not totally unconnected, surely, were Cheetham's weekly *Journal* advertisements as agent for the Gramophone & Typewriter Company's 'genuine gramophones', complete with endorsements by Patti, Melba and Lauder. In truth, the September 'invitation' concert had been held with the object of 'introducing some of the latest makes in gramophones to public notice'!

The 'thrilling fire scene and rescue' screened during two successive weeks in August presented music in a novel manner. Whether it was one of the numerous 'fire' films screened by Cheetham over the years or a new one, it was complemented by music-hall singer Hamilton Hill's 'famous "Fireman's Song"'. Australian-born Hill had recorded it for one of Gaumont's innovative 'Chronophone' films, in which performers were simultaneously seen on screen and heard on disc. It is not clear whether Cheetham's combination incorporated a record of

Hill or a 'live' rendition. In whatever form it was presented, its single verse was followed by the rousing chorus: 'Fire, Fire, Fire. The fire brigade is coming / There's a clatter of hoofs as they rush by, / a battle with flames that reach sky high. / Fire, Fire, Fire, see the crowd a-running / And as they draw near, here's a rousing cheer! / Hoorah! for the lads of the fire brigade'. Hamilton Hill can be heard singing *The Fireman's Song* on *YouTube*.

1906 at the Central Hall ended on a high note. People were turned away on the last three Saturdays, with packed houses being the norm during Christmas week. Early in December, the *Journal* reported that Cheetham had obtained a long lease on the venue, enabling him to re-arrange much of the seating without interfering with performances. By mid-February 1907, crimson plush seats costing a shilling (5p in today's money but corresponding to more than £5, considering inflation) had been installed in the front stalls and blue tip-up sixpennies (2½p today) in the centre, with fourpennies at the sides. Admission to the newly-erected 200-seat gallery cost thruppence. And in March 1907 the *Journal* commented favourably on the seating, the décor and 'the general comfort and warmth on cold nights' in what had become Rhyl's first permanent cinema.

Films mentioned in this chapter which can be viewed on *YouTube*: *The Train Wreckers (1905 film)* (Edison), *The Great Train Robbery 1903* (Edison), *Les Dévaliseurs noctunes / Burglars at work* (Pathé) and *Grandma's Reading Glass* (Smith)

On the East Anglian Film Archive's website: *Rescued in Mid Air* (Alpha)

Gramophone and phonograph recordings of Hamilton Hill singing *The Fireman's Song* can be heard on *YouTube* by googling 'The Fireman's Song' and 'Hamilton Hill'

Chapter 13

1907–1912: *Later Films*

In spite of being busy with his cinemas in Rhyl, Aberystwyth and Colwyn Bay Arthur Cheetham managed to produce at least eleven films between 1907 and 1912. Apart from a comedy and a specially-commissioned publicity production they were all topicals, shot mainly at Rhyl.

A signboard projecting over the pavement outside his Central Hall cinema and a fire in town provided him with filming opportunities in 1907. The 'signboard' story has been related by the film-maker himself in his 1908 weekly programme-booklet, by daughter Gwen during her 1977 interview and by both local newspapers. The *Record and Advertiser* describes it as 'an interesting scene not devoid of an element of humour', and the *Journal* calls it 'A Signboard Comedy'. While the fire was reported at length by both papers, the story of Cheetham's filming of the event can be found mainly in his 1908 publication.

Cheetham justifies the signboard on the grounds that his cinema was in a side-street, that visitors had difficulty in finding the entrance and that it was 'not an ordinary place of business, but a place of Entertainment and a boon to the town'. Nevertheless, he acknowledges that, after starting to erect it, he had been informed verbally by the Council Clerk that prior permission was required. So while submitting a formal application, he continued provocatively with the work 'so that the real design … could be seen' and undertook to take it down 'the very moment everyone else in the Town was treated in the same way'. The Council reacted decisively by sending men armed with ladders and poles to remove it. Cheetham had expected them at 8.30 am, but they were discovered at work much earlier. He started filming the proceedings and threatened to sue for trespass unless the ladders were removed. They explained that they were only obeying orders. But work seems to have stopped for a while, since one explanatory caption in the resultant film declares: 'The men go away to consult the Town Surveyor'.

Work is resumed. So filming is resumed, capturing an incident introduced by the caption: 'A donkey shies at a scaffold pole'. Although the two-wheeled cart drawn by the supposedly startled creature spins around in the street, the driver doesn't appear to lose control. So it is difficult to tell whether the manœuvre is effected by man or by beast – or whether the incident has been choreographed by Cheetham. Councillors eventually arrive and, seeing that the workmen have failed to dislodge the signboard, order them to stop.

During the film's Saturday premier at the Central Hall, the aggrieved proprietor related the whole story to date. His camera then captured the audience filing out into the street at the end of the show. This sequence was added to the film for screening during the following week.

The *Record and Advertiser* anticipated that the next move would be made in court. About a week later, however, the council workmen returned at dead of night. Cheetham was alerted, confronted them at about 3 am and had words with the Council Surveyor. But he made no effort to obstruct the successful removal of the signboard.

A few hours later a crowd collected in Market Street to see that the signboard had been replaced by a huge banner bearing the words: 'In Memoriam. Sacred to the memory of a signboard taken down in the middle of the night by the Rhyl Urban District Council. "For men loved darkness rather than light, because their deeds were evil." John III, 19'. According to Mrs Gwen Cordery, her mother had provided the closing riposte because 'she had been a Sunday School teacher and knew her Bible'. Finally, Cheetham printed a poster which read: 'The board above was taken down by the Rhyl Urban District Council. This is how they treat an enterprising man in Rhyl'. He completed the film with a shot of an employee, brush in hand, pasting it onto the cinema wall.

Cheetham's version of the story reiterates his sense of victimisation: 'no other signs have been removed either by owners or the Council before or after the Central Hall Episode'. Nevertheless, other captions in the film such as 'STRONG REINFORCEMENTS OF SCAFFOLD POLES, &c.', 'End of Act 1. – Retreat.' and 'AFTER BREAKFAST The men return – It must come down.' reveal him as having a decidedly dry sense of humour. The film's survival as a series of discontinuous fragments is dealt with in Chapter 16.

The Queen's Palace opened on the Promenade in August 1902. In addition to a theatre/ballroom, its attractions comprised 'a faithful reproduction in miniature of Venice' in the basement with 'real gondolas' to ride in and 'real Italians' to steer them, shopping arcade, waxwork tableaux, picture gallery, shooting gallery, roof garden and an electric lift ascending to the 'crow's nest' above the tower and glass-covered dome affording 'a magnificent panorama of the surrounding scenery'.

Films would augment the live 'turns' of the venue's variety shows. In August 1903 one of those screened by Jack Barnes's

'Royal American Bioscope pictures ... direct from St James' Hall, London' featured a motor-car race held in Ireland in July and sponsored by Gordon Bennett, owner of the *New York Herald Tribune*. It had been covered by five English film producers.

The films screened in 1904 and 1905 were advertised as 'Vivigraph'. Local newspaper reports such as 'seems to improve every week' and 'New pictures of an interesting and amusing character' indicate that, like the live 'turns', they were changed regularly. 'Vivigraph' was changed to 'Palagraph' (based, clearly, on the venue's name) in 1907. But the season was ended abruptly by a fire in the building. Arthur Cheetham was on hand to film it.

The *Record and Advertiser*'s report on the fire begins by noting that Rhyl had suffered a combination of thunder, lightning, rain, hail and a strong north-westerly gale throughout the night of Saturday 23 November. At about 7 am on the Sunday, photographer John Williams smelt smoke from his High Street studio. He ran to the police station to raise the alarm. The Superintendent rang the fire bell, which was heard all over town. The local fire brigade soon arrived, followed by their counterparts from nearby Rhuddlan, Prestatyn and Abergele. The firemen battled with smoke and fire all day, the flames being fanned by the continuing gale. They faced danger as they clambered on roofs, while walls collapsed around them and red-hot débris rained down. Mercifully, there were only two injuries: one fireman was hit on the head, and a young helper broke a leg when a wall collapsed. Both were taken to hospital.

When John Williams raised the alarm the building was well alight, but the staff and visitors at the adjoining Queen's Hotel escaped unharmed. The *Record and Advertiser* reported that 'the glass [of the dome] could not hold out long against such a powerful blaze [and] it succumbed. In quick succession pane after pane ... cracked and fell both inside and out. The flames ... leapt high into the air ... and this was certainly a most magnificent yet awful spectacle'. The crowd who had gathered on the Promenade were warned to keep well back as the dome and the tower 'began to move slowly towards the sea, and fell somewhat leisurely into the roadway'.

'Fortunately', writes Cheetham in typical third-person self-adulatory style, 'Mr. Cheetham had some unexposed negative cinematographic film in stock and he at once brought out his camera and trained it on the burning building. Animated Pictures were thus taken of the great fire in its various stages, and from various positions. It required some endurance to stand there and take these pictures in the teeth of what was practically a blizzard'. Premiered at the Central Hall on the following Tuesday, the film was loyally described by the *Journal* as 'showing up finely the rolling clouds of smoke, which is an impossible thing in the ordinary photograph'.

Cheetham refers to extra footage he added to the film: a practice fire-brigade turnout at the beginning and 'an animated portrait picture of the Brigade ... as a finale'. He agreed to his London agent's request to put the film (of the loss of a popular attraction!) on the general market, as 'a great advertisement for Rhyl'. *Fire at Palace, Rhyl* was duly advertised by the Warwick Trading Company in the 12 December issue of the *Kinematograph Weekly*.

'It will not be out of place here', concludes Cheetham, 'to record [that] Mr Cheetham gave a special BENEFIT for the members of the Fire Brigade, devoting the takings of both houses, without any deductions whatever, for any expenses of any kind'. The total came to £9. The film hasn't survived, but the work of local photographers has and provides arresting evidence of the event. One view of the falling dome and tower was reproduced both as a picture-postcard and a hand-coloured lantern slide.

A sad postscript to the fire story was the letter from Arthur Rowlands, honorary secretary of Rhyl Fire Brigade (a voluntary organisation) published by the local papers in the following August. It appealed for donations to Thomas Roberts, the young helper who had been injured. He was unable to resume work, having been a patient at a Liverpool hospital at his parents' expense. He had received £7 from the local council, £5 from the directors of the Palace Company, ten shillings (50p in to-day's money) from the benefit film-show and £1 2s 0d (one pound and two shillings) from members of the fire brigade.

On a lighter note: a few weeks after the fire the *Journal* published the efforts deemed 'best' in a limerick competition at a Town Hall whist-drive. Among them was 'There was a nice Palace in Rhyl, / With a tower as high as a hill; / But one day in November / 'Twas burnt to a cinder – / But it's helped Cheetham's coffers to fill'. The Queen's Palace, including most of the shopping arcade, was destroyed in the fire but it was rebuilt (*sans* dome) as the Queen's Theatre, which remained open until 1960.

Arthur Cheetham produced four films in 1908, all of them in Rhyl. The first depicted yet another May Day procession and was screened at the Central Hall during Whit-week. Also on the programme was the 1907 fire film 'for the benefit of the visitors, who', observed the *Journal*, 'will, no doubt, be much interested in the vivid reproduction of the destruction of the Queen's Palace'.

On Thursday 30 July the local council's new Pavilion Theatre opened on the Promenade. Cheetham had shot two films on site in March: work in progress and local dignitaries laying foundation stones. The first was screened at his cinema throughout the following week. But the second, sent to London to be developed and printed, was mislaid *en route*. After he complained about his 'lavish expense on telegrams, &c., &c.' the missing parcel was traced and delivered, and the film was screened a week later than planned.

Wednesday 1 July saw the inauguration of a daily non-stop summer train service leaving Euston at 11.15 am and arriving at Rhyl at 3.20 pm. The arrival of Friday 17 July was a special occasion. The stationmaster and the town's Advertising Association had arranged for it to be photographed for the *Daily Mirror*. The *Journal* reported that a large crowd of councillors, Association members and ministers of religion had gathered on the platform several minutes before the train was due. It continued: 'Our enterprising townsman and entertainer, Mr A Cheetham, was busy with his cinematograph camera, and obtained an excellent series of pictures of the train and the crowd'. The train arrives. Then, presumably for the benefit of *Daily Mirror* readers, a sign is attached to the front of the engine standing at the platform to announce that Rhyl was the first stop on this special service. Finally, the camera is trained on the milling crowd of dignitaries, passengers, sightseers and station staff on the platform before capturing the train's departure for Colwyn Bay. Almost a minute of the film survives, much marred by decomposition.

In October the *Journal* reported on a revival of Cheetham's annual tour, to 'a number of excellent residential towns north of London'. The Queen's Palace fire film figured prominently, and 'Rhyl Palace Fire' had been printed in large letters on the posters. It was hoped that the handbills, circulars etc prepared for the tour would prove to be 'a great advantage for the town'.

Arthur Cheetham is not known as a producer of dramas or comedies, although a short film about boys upsetting a market-trader's cart can be attributed to him on grounds of provenance (as explained in Chapter 16). However, the *Journal* for 30 January 1909 adjudged his Central Hall programme for the following week to be 'thoroughly abreast of the times', in respect not only of a film about a recent Italian earthquake but also of his own new comedy *A Motor Mystery*. It was about self-styled heiress Violet Charlesworth, who lived at nearby St Asaph. Renowned for her extravagant lifestyle and love of fast cars, she claimed dishonestly that she would inherit a considerable fortune on her impending 25th birthday.

On 2 January she drove to the precipitous Penmaen-bach headland on the north Wales coast, about 20 miles west of Rhyl. Her sister and chauffeur were with her. They both claimed that she had been thrown through the windscreen and down the cliff. But their testimony was a complete fabrication, and she was found safe and sound in Oban about a fortnight later. It is difficult to imagine how this escapade had been re-enacted for the screen as a comedy. But the *Rhyl Journal* insisted that it was 'one of the most screamingly funny animated pictures ever seen'. As to its production: a *Rhyl and North Wales Weekly News* advertisement for Cheetham's Colwyn Bay cinema in February 1912 emphasised that the crucial scene had been shot 'at the exact spot where the "supposed" accident took place'.

The story was widely reported, even making the pages of the *New York Times*. Another film, entitled *The Welsh Cliff Mystery* and featuring Charlesworth herself, was shot by

Joseph Rosenthal (of Boer War film fame) for Ruffell's Imperial Bioscope Syndicate of Westminster.[1] Although denying any connection between her disappearance and her considerable debts, she was obliged to pay her creditors 75% of the income from her 'celebrity' music-hall appearances and screenings of *The Welsh Cliff Mystery*. In the following year she and her mother were found guilty of obtaining money by fraud, false pretences and conspiracy on matters unrelated to her disappearance, and imprisoned.[2]

Within a week of its September 1910 opening, Cheetham's Aberystwyth cinema was screening a film entitled *The Weekly Animated Chronicle*. Among its 'world's happenings day by day' was recent storm damage to the town's promenade. The *Cambrian News* forecast: 'this picture will be shown in scores of large towns and should prove a big advertisement for Aberystwyth as a seaside resort'. Whether or not Cheetham shot this local item, he certainly had the means of doing so, however unsuitable it might be for attracting visitors.

1911 saw the production of Cheetham's fourth and final Rhyl May Day film. Reporting on 'a special view [for] a selected company', the *Record and Advertiser* observed that the participants in the procession were easily recognised and declared it proof 'that a large number of competitors after receiving their prize cards did not negotiate the whole route as

---

[1] At that time Ruffell's Imperial Bioscope Syndicate were film renters, but would also be dealing in 'apparatus' in 1910 and branching out into film production, the manufacture of automatic pianos, magic lanterns etc by about 1913 (*The London Project, the birth of the film business in London*, on-line)

[2] Jon Burrows. 'Melodrama of the dear old kind: Sentimentalising British action heroines in the 1910s' in *Film History*, vol 18, 2006. Pages 166-9 and 172 deal with London and suburban newspaper coverage of Charlesworth's music-hall appearances and Rosenthal's film

laid down in the rules of the May Day committee'. One wonders how the guilty reacted to this exposure when the film was screened at the Central Hall.

Cheetham was also busy filming at Aberystwyth that year, both in connection with a visit by newly-crowned King George V and Queen Mary and to promote the town as a seaside resort. The royal pair, accompanied by the Prince of Wales (fresh from his investiture at Caernarfon Castle) and the Princess Royal, were there to lay the Welsh National Library's twin foundation stones. After appending their signatures to what the *Cambrian News* called the Library's autograph book, all four were escorted to a temporary pavilion, where invited guests were seated. Members of the general public stood outside. According to the *Rhyl Journal*, 'Mr Cheetham had exclusive permission to take cinematograph pictures of the ceremony' and shot 'a series of pictures from three different positions' during the day. His camera had an unrestricted view of the stone-laying.

The National Screen and Sound Archive of Wales holds a copy of Pathé's film *Aberystwyth. The King and Queen Accompanied by the Prince of Wales and Princess Mary* [the Princess Royal] *Perform a Stone-laying Ceremony*. Each stone had been lowered into place by block-and-tackle before being formally 'laid' by King and Queen in turn. In the first scene of the surviving half-minute of the film the Queen taps her stone formally with a mallet several times, with her uniformed husband in attendance. She is then seen examining the plans of the proposed library watched by King, Prince and Princess.

The stone-laying took place on Saturday 15 July. The *Rhyl Journal* reported that the negative of Cheetham's film left Aberystwyth for London at 6 pm (presumably by train) and 'notwithstanding that no Sunday labour was indulged in' the positive print arrived in time to be screened at his New Market Hall cinema on the Monday evening. The attention accorded to his film and the exclusivity claimed for it suggest that it could have been one and the same as Pathé's better-known coverage of the event. Whatever the truth, this was the third and final time for Arthur Cheetham to train his ciné camera on the royal couple successively known as Duke and Duchess of Cornwall and York, Prince and Princess of Wales and King George V and Queen Mary – as he proudly pointed out in the booklet celebrating the opening of his Colwyn Bay cinema in the December of that year.

As to his second Aberystwyth film of 1911: Cheetham entrusted the management of his Rhyl cinema for some weeks to son Gustavus and the 'musical arrangements' to Bernard. Their father, reported the *Journal*, was 'engaged in taking a series of cinematograph pictures for the Aberystwyth Corporation, for the purpose of advertising the town'. Incidentally, when the *Welsh Coast Pioneer* referred to this film's screening on the Colwyn Bay cinema's opening day, it quoted Cheetham as announcing that it had already been seen in Birmingham, Chester 'and other English centres attracting favourable Press notices'.

On 25 July 1909, French aeronaut Louis Blériot made the first crossing of the English Channel in what was then called a 'heavier-than-air machine'. But the Irish Sea remained unconquered, and Arthur Cheetham's last documented film featured the attempt of 24-year-old Vivian Hewitt in 1912. Hewitt hailed from a wealthy Grimsby brewing family. His father had insisted that he should be able to earn a living, so he was sent to work at Portsmouth Dockyard and the L&NWR works in Crewe after leaving Harrow. He then became a dealer in second-hand cars and aeroplanes at the newly-opened Brooklands racing circuit in Surrey. He also learned to fly, eventually becoming a popular exhibition aeronaut. By 1912 he was living in Rhyl, where he had his own landing-field and hangar.

On Friday 26 April, Hewitt and his Blériot monoplane were in a field near Holyhead, waiting for the weather to improve. Although he knew that his rival, Irishman Denis Corbett-Wilson, had just completed the shorter southern crossing from Pembrokeshire, the challenge of the longest flight over water beckoned. Arthur Cheetham was there. Writing later in his *Rhyl Pilot*, he describes the excited crowd waiting for hours, the painstaking examination and preparation of the aeroplane and his filming of 'the young ladies and others [who] came to Mr Hewitt asking for his autograph'. He considered 'both humorous and picturesque' the scene when some of the 'yokels' were asked to hold the machine while the engine was being tested. Their caps were blown off their heads, and the grass was flattened. At last, on take-off: 'It was a glorious and beautiful sight to see the machine rise so gracefully, soar round in a beautiful curve, and gradually disappear out of sight'. Several days later, after a successful flight, Hewitt returned to Rhyl from Dublin by sea and rail to be carried shoulder-high through the streets in a torchlight procession to a hero's welcome at the Town Hall.

Cheetham had experienced difficulty in training his camera on the aeroplane as it took off, sped away at 50 mph and climbed to some 2,000 feet within seconds. Back at his Rhyl cinema, however, the film was found to be a success when projected on the screen. He printed a handbill bearing Hewitt's photograph and signature and proudly announcing: 'The Animated Picture of VIVIAN HEWITT'S FLIGHT TO

IRELAND is the sole copyright of Mr. A. Cheetham, who Cinematographed the Flight, and this Picture can only be seen at the MARKET STREET Cinema, Rhyl'. But he supplied a copy to the Topical Film Company for their twice-weekly *Topical Budget* newsreel. The company's archive has been deposited with the National Film Archive in London, but no 1912 issues have survived.[3]

Films mentioned in this chapter which can be viewed on *YouTube*: *Gordon Bennett Motor Race (1903)* (British Pathé and Huntley Film Archives)

On *'Britain on Film' BFI Player*: *First Through Train from Euston to Rhyl, 1908* (Cheetham)

On *YouTube*, but not mentioned in the chapter: *La traversée de la Manche, Louis Bleriot, 1909*. In spite of the title (The English Channel Crossing), it merely shows a Blériot take-off followed by a trial flight

---

[3] *Modest Millionaire*, William Hywel's biography of Hewitt, deals with Blériot's 1906 flight, Hewitt's background and Holyhead/Dublin flight, Corbett-Wilson and Cheetham's film. But the story of the young aeronaut's triumphal return to Rhyl is more complicated than this chapter's brief treatment suggests

Chapter 14

Music and More

Several songs sung by Arthur Cheetham, his wife and guest performers in his film-shows between 1897 and 1899 were highlighted in the previews, advertisements and reports which appeared in both local papers. Illustrated by lantern slides, they typify the heroic, moralistic and religious fare placed before Victorian audiences. It is not surprising to find that one of them was in Welsh, considering that it was sung during an out-of-season evening's entertainment in a seaside town where about half the population were fluent in the language.

The words of *The Village Blacksmith*, sung by T. Amos Jones in 1897, are by Henry Wadsworth Longfellow. Its eight verses extol the subject's work-ethic and proclaim him metaphorically to be an exemplar 'at the flaming forge of life'. Seven of them, sung by Derek B. Scott, Professor of Critical Musicology at the University of Leeds to his own piano accompaniment, can be heard on-line on the *Victorian Web literature, history and culture in the age of Victoria*. According to Professor Scott, the music, composed by Liverpool-born bass singer Willoughby Hunter Weiss, provides a dramatic musical setting.

Also sung by T. Amos Jones in 1897 was *Y Bachgen Dewr* (The Brave Boy). Published bilingually and entitled *The Noble Boy of Truth* in English, its words are by Montgomeryshire poet Robert Davies, writing under the *nom de plume* of *Mynyddog*. Dr Joseph Parry, who composed the music, is renowned for his numerous hymn-tunes, the music of the opera *Blodwen* and the celebrated song of unrequited love

Myfanwy (words of both by Davies). The *Bachgen Dewr* is a young stowaway who is discovered on board ship by the captain. Boy insists that his father has hidden him there. Captain threatens him but is eventually convinced of his innocence by his fervent prayer. The song concludes with the captain's heartfelt avowal of respect for God and an exhortation to speak and love the truth everywhere: *A dysgwn ninnau ym mhob man i ddweud a charu'r gwir.*

The Better Land, sung by Mme Marie Williamson in 1897, was written by Felicia Dorothea Hemans. As a discourse on the contemporary prevalence of infant mortality, it is addressed to the bereaved. 'Is it [the Better Land] where the flower of the orange blows?' she asks. Or 'where the feathery palm-trees rise?' Or ''midst the green islands of glittering seas?' Or 'where the rivers wander o'er sands of gold?' 'Not there', she replies every time, concluding: 'Eye hath not seen it … ear hath not heard its deep songs of joy', because it is 'far beyond the clouds, and beyond the tomb.'

Anchored, sung by Mrs Cheetham in 1898, is a dramatic ballad by Samuel K. Cowan, with music by Michael Watson. Its 'sailor lad' voyages through summer sea, gale and storm, buoyed up by the hope of being 'safe in my father's home' after 'only another day to stray, only another night to roam' – a hope dashed in purely earthly terms, considering both the condition of his ship and the poem's religious symbolism. Professor Scott also sings this song on the *Victorian Web literature, history and culture in the age of Victoria.* He considers that the composer has made use of strong musical contrasts, drawing upon operatic techniques to depict moods.

Also sung by Mrs Cheetham in 1898 was the religious ballad *The Holy City.* With words by Frederic Weatherby and music by Michael Maybrick, it takes its inspiration from the prophecy in *Revelations* XXI, 2: 'I John saw the holy city, new Jerusalem, coming down from God out of heaven'. In the opening lines: 'Last night I lay a sleeping / There came a dream so fair, / I stood in old Jerusalem / Beside the temple there'. The city then becomes 'hushed' by the Crucifixion and finally transformed triumphantly into 'the new Jerusalem that would not pass away'. Harry Secombe and the Mormon Tabernacle Choir are among those who can be heard singing *The Holy City* on *YouTube*.

The Little Hero, sung by Cheetham during his 1899 benefit concert, tells the story of another stowaway. His father has told him that the ship would take him to 'Halifax town so far'. But he is discovered by the 'bit-of-a-savage' first mate. In spite of the boy's pleading: 'Then the mate pulled his watch from his pocket / just as if he's been drawing his knife. / 'If in ten minutes more you don't tell, lad, / there's the rope and "good-bye" to dear life'. But like the captain in *Y Bachgen Dewr*, he is impressed by the boy's sincerity and relents. The words of *The Little Hero* are by Arthur Matthison, set to music by singer Stephen Adams, who became publisher Boosey's most popular composer by the end of the 1880s. Professor Scott also sings this song on the *Victorian Web literature, history and culture in the age of Victoria*.

Henry Théodore Pontet's *The Toilers* (sung twice by Mrs Cheetham in 1898) asks the 'happy ones of this fair earth, while gathered round [their] glowing hearths' to think of the coalminers and fishermen who risk life and limb to provide them with home comforts and sustenance. A set of lantern slides was produced by Bamforths in 1897 to illustrate this song. All fourteen can be viewed on the Magic Lantern Society's website.

Bearing in mind the nature of *The Village Blacksmith, Y Bachgen Dewr, The Better Land, Anchored, The Holy City, The*

Little Hero and *The Toilers, Daddie* (sung by Mme Williamson in 1897) is likely to have engendered similar emotions in her audience, rather than being the light-hearted *Daddie Wouldn't Buy Me a Bow Wow*, written by English songwriter Joseph Tabrar for music-hall singer/comedienne Vesta Victoria.

Gramophone records had been part of Cheetham's film-shows since his introduction of 'the Latest American Loud-speaking Talking Machine' in 1898. Following the *Messiah* concerts of November and December 1906, two different songs from the oratorio were to be played daily in the intervals between films in the new year – a project which the *Journal* reckoned would take about a fortnight to complete!

Records were often played during Cheetham's post-1906 cinema days at Rhyl, typically described by the *Journal* as: 'a remarkably fine series of gramophone selections' (1907), 'items by Battistini and other famous vocalists … reproduced with as much reality as though the artistes themselves were present' (1908), 'delightful gramophone reproductions … of the finest music ever heard, both vocal and instrumental' (1909), 'the choicest gramophone selections' (1910) and 'the new gramophone records … of the pianoforte selections by the great Paderewski' (1911). One notable event of February 1908 was the 'Grand Afternoon Concert on the Melba Gramophone'. The first part comprised selections from Mendelssohn's *Elijah*, and the second included new recordings by Italian *coloratura* soprano Luisa Tetrazzina.

Cheetham continued to sell gramophones and records until 1913, when a *Journal* advertisement for his 'sensational sale … commencing 10am, Saturday March 1st' announced that he was giving up that part of his business. It does not seem to have been an instant success, since the advertisement was repeated several times in March and April. But in 1907, while he was still local agent of the Gramophone & Typewriter Company, it had been suggested to him that Rhyl should host one of their gramophone concerts held in aid of the Lord Mayor of London's 'Cripples' fund for the treatment at a Hampshire hospital of children suffering from tuberculosis of the bones or joints.

However, Cheetham persuaded the company to adopt Rhyl's Royal Alexandra Hospital as beneficiary and booked the Town Hall for 3 pm and 8 pm on Thursday 7 November. While recordings of Patti, Melba, Caruso etc were being played, their lantern-slide 'portraits' were projected on the screen. Towards the end of the evening concert Cheetham appeared on stage and announced ('to applause') that the day's takings amounted to £23 11s 2d (23 pounds, eleven shillings and tuppence). But, he added, £2 was deductable for the rent of the hall, unless the councillors thought fit to 'remit' the charge. But the cheque received in due course by the hospital amounted to precisely £21 11s 2d!

In 1912 Cheetham reverted to his earlier practice of augmenting films with live performers – but as 'an addition to and not as a substitution of any part of the programme'. Consequently, his twice-nightly Monday-to-Friday 'houses' were reduced to single ones, with afternoon matinees on Mondays, Thursdays and Saturdays. For 14 weeks between March and June he engaged a wide range of 'artistes' – vocalists (including a lady who sang to her own 'cello *obligato* accompaniment); a flute-and-piccolo player; comedians (one duo was called 'Whitty and Wise'); performing dogs (in Madame Rousseau's case, her 'smallest toy dogs in the world' all fitted onto a table-top); a 'London Society entertainer' with his 'sketches, songs and imitations'; Japanese illusionists; a character actor presenting 'sketches from Dickens and from other plays [sic]'; a magician/escapologist who conjured up cigars, cigarettes, chocolate, fruit etc for distribution among the audience; and a ventriloquist who obligingly varied his performance in order to conform to the Thursday change of film.

There were no more press references to Gus Cheetham's participation in his father's shows after the Whit-week of 1904, or of Bernard's after February 1906. But one 1910 issue of the *Journal* mentions 'the musical selections [whether 'live' or on gramophone records] with which the pictures are interspersed, and sometimes accompanied'. Exceptionally, however, in July 1914 the paper credited 'the music accompaniment to the show of pictures' to a Miss Topping, 'who has a very fine touch, and whose playing adds greatly to the attraction provided at the cinema'.

Professor Derek B. Scott can be heard singing *The Village Blacksmith, Anchored* and *The Little Hero* on the *Victorian Web literature, history and culture in the age of Victoria* by googling each title, followed by 'Derek B. Scott'

Bamforth's *The Toilers* lantern slides can be viewed by googling 'The Toilers – The Magic Lantern Society' and selecting 'Associated slide set: *The toilers*'. By courtesy of *Lucerna Magic Lantern Web Resource, www.slides.uni.trier.de/slide/index. php?id=5004553. Accessed 12 April 2017*

Chapter 15

'The Firm'

Preceding chapters lend credence to film historian David Berry's descriptions of Arthur Cheetham as a 'sometime "quack", incorrigible self-publicist' and 'flamboyant entrepreneur', not to mention 'grandstanding maverick' (which he shared with his audience during the 2007 Welsh Screen Classics Film Festival in Aberystwyth). Personality apart, however, this resourceful businessman owed much to his family for his success. A lantern slide wishing patrons 'the compliments of the season' depicts not only Cheetham but also his wife, sons Gustavus and Bernard and daughters Frances, Edith and Gwen.

It was Gwen who, as elderly Mrs Cordery, identified soloist Madame Rose Garton as none other than her mother. But Mrs Cheetham had also typed out her husband's 'character delineations', 'capably managed' the 1902-03 tour and supplied the biblical quotation during the 1907 signboard affair. Mrs Cordery also related how she herself would sell gramophone records, fold and staple copies of *The Rhyl Pilot* and sell tickets at the Rhyl, Colwyn Bay and Aberystwyth cinemas.

The 1911 Colwyn Bay booklet eulogises the sons as 'cradled in the business ... having grown up with it since the beginning of Cinematography in this country'. Both had occasionally 'taken entire charge and management of tours'. Bernard was at that time 'Operator [projectionist] at Mr. Cheetham's Rhyl Theatre'. Being 'a natural mechanic', Gustavus had 'entirely wired and fitted the Electrical Installation' at Rhyl and organised 'the mechanical and electrical equipment of each Theatre'. He was also responsible for 'arranging the Programmes, and ... supervising the selection of the Pictures ... so that nothing shall be shown that is in the slightest manner objectionable'.[1]

The *Record and Advertiser*'s report on Gustavus's wedding at Rhyl in 1913 describes him as managing the Rhyl cinema. When Bernard married at Aberystwyth in the following year, the *Cambrian News* noted that he was resident manager of his father's cinema there. On the sons' return from war service in early 1919 Cheetham Sr retired and made them joint proprietors of the Rhyl cinema. Within weeks, however, it was taken over by 22-year-old local businessman Derek Shannon. Among his innovations were the *circa* 1920 local newsreels to be mentioned briefly in Chapter 16.

Arthur Cheetham then set off for Los Angeles, accompanied by his wife and daughters Gwen and Edith. A *Kinematograph Weekly* tribute to him entitled 'A Pioneer of Cinematography' recalled the days when 'a hundred feet of film was looked upon as "something wonderful and marvelous" '. His intention, it was understood, in '[bidding] farewell to the trade in England [sic]' was '[to] continue his active connection with the business'. But in his 1998 interview Stanley Cheetham insisted that his grandfather was merely going on holiday, adding that one unforeseen consequence was that Edith married and settled in the States. But for decades to follow, the words painted in black on the brickwork of the Rhyl cinema's gable wall served as a reminder of Arthur Cheetham's lengthy association with the venue. By the 1970s, however, even the prominent 'SILVOGRAPH' and 'PROPRIETOR. A. CHEETHAM.' had all but disappeared. They are now covered

---

[1] *Opening of the Colwyn Bay Cinema in connection with Arthur Cheetham's Picture Theatres.* [1911], pp. [13]-[14]: National Library of Wales

by the pebble-dash which protects the walls of the whole building.

Stanley Cheetham had teenage recollections of the cinema trade's respect for his grandfather in the early 1930s, when he was presented with an illuminated address by the Cinematograph Exhibitors' Association. Filming eventually passed to the next generation. Aberystwyth events of the 1920s covered by son Gustavus feature boys' walking races, the unveiling of the local war memorial, school folk-dancing and gymnastics and a 'coll v town' race. They all survive, and the story of their discovery is related in Chapter 16. The 'coll v town' film, celebrating the inauguration of the Aberystwyth Town Harriers, provides a rare opportunity to see footage of Rhyl's pioneer film-maker. There he is, holding the crowd back at the finishing line to provide camera-man Gustavus with an unrestricted view of the runners.

Aspects of Arthur Cheetham the family man are revealed by the concerns and hopes he expresses in a letter to a nephew on his way to military service in India soon after the outbreak of World War I. A photocopy of it was proudly shown to me by a distant relative of the film-maker at one of my local history classes in Rhyl some years ago. Thinking of the sub-continent's climate, he recommends total abstinence: 'if you should get any alcohol in your rations, and they will allow you to have something else in place of it – you should get that "something else" and you will do yourself untold good'. He confidently expects 'great things' from his nephew and suggests: 'if you keep your eyes open, use your wits, and study well, I see no reason why you should not come back with an officer's rank of some sort'. Appealing to his sense of duty, he enjoins him to follow the advice of 'your noble commander, Lord Kitchener, who asks you to let the world know that the British Soldier is a GENTLEMAN'. And, although 'it is very unlikely now that you will see any active service, as you are going to Bombay [Mumbai] but if you do, I know that you will be **brave**, even to recklessness'. Finally, before signing off as 'Your loving uncle': 'be so upright and true and your mother and your wife will be proud of you – and in that pride we shall all have a share'.

Arthur Cheetham's final residence was at Withington, Manchester. He died in January 1937 at a Hertfordshire health farm just weeks after his wife passed away. Considering his long and intimate association with Rhyl, it is surprising to find that his *North Wales Weekly News* obituary is much longer than that in the *Rhyl Journal*. Although the latter refers to him as cinema proprietor, phrenologist, electrical treatment expert and printer, it emphasises his period as a 'lively' member of Rhyl Urban District Council who had been 'more than once in conflict with the Council in connection with the administration of certain bylaws'. This remark brings to mind not only the 1907 signboard affair but also a similar one in 1910, when he was a councillor. A fellow-member mentioned complaints about 'an over-hanging sign' the cinema proprietor had set up **across** Market Street. During the ensuing exchange Cheetham referred to 1907 and asked why his sign was the only one to be removed since. New ones had been erected without Council permission, he insisted, and no notification had been sent to the owners. Nevertheless, he undertook to observe the full letter of the law and seems to have done so, since no further mention was made of the matter in the local press. As grandson Stanley put it: 'he was good at annoying the council'.

Films mentioned in this chapter which can be viewed on *'Britain on Film' BFI Player*: *Boys' Walking Races*; *Unveiling of Aberystwyth War Memorial*; *Aberystwyth County School Gymnastic Display* and *First Road Race. Coll v Town Inaugurating the Aberystwyth Town Harriers* (all by Gustavus Cheetham)

Chapter 16

'two separate collections of films in dusty cans'

This chapter's title is David Berry's imaginative depiction of Arthur Cheetham's cinematic legacy. The 'two separate collections' typify the 'lucky dip' nature of ensuring the survival of early films. As far as Cheetham's output is concerned, I 'dipped' both luckily and twice – though not on the same scale as Peter Worden and Robin Whalley with the Mitchell and Kenyon collection in Blackburn.

The nitro-cellulose transparent base of ciné film used in Cheetham's day ignites at 130°C (226°F), burns quickly and is explosive in large quantities. Deterioration of the image begins at the moment of production, but can be retarded by storage at optimum conditions of temperature and relative humidity together with adequate ventilation. Fortunately, however, nearly all Cheetham's surviving films were still in acceptable condition without needing such attention when they were saved for posterity in the late 20th century by being copied onto stable acetyl-cellulose 'masters' before transfer to film, video-cassette or DVD as appropriate for viewing.

I first read about Arthur Cheetham in J.W. Jones's *Rhyl, the Town and its People,* published by the author in 1970. This local historian was arguably the first person to bring Rhyl's pioneer film-maker to serious public attention. Then, in early 1973, I was invited to address Rhyl Rotary Club on my appointment as warden of the town's newly-opened teachers' centre. After my talk, Glyndwr Richards, head of the primary school adjoining the centre, introduced me to his fellow-member and retired Rhyl businessman Eric Foulkes, who told me about his collection of local films and invited me to view them at his home. I accepted gladly, particularly since my brief at the centre included the production of local history resources for schools.

During my subsequent visit Mr Foulkes manned an antiquated projector placed on the lounge floor and proceeded to treat me to a magical black-and-white tour of old Rhyl on a make-shift screen propped up against a chair. Whatever else I was shown that evening, I vividly remember the 1903 May Day film, with children and dogs weaving their way unconcernedly through the cavalcade of horse-drawn vehicles. Realising that I was suitably impressed, my host offered me his collection there and then. Although totally lacking in experience of film conservation, I felt obliged to accept and resolved not to betray his trust in me.

Eric Foulkes's collection of Cheetham films ranged from 1899 to 1907 and comprised nine out of the surviving 12 unequivocally acknowledged as shot by the Rhyl pioneer. 1899 was represented by the royal visit to Conwy and the Merrie Men; 1902 by the 'British' and 'National' schoolchildren; 1903 by the May Day procession, Buffalo Bill and the Cycling Club outing; and 1907 by the 'Signboard Comedy' fragments (which I later converted selectively into a set of 35mm transparencies maintaining the thrust of the story). Also in his collection were local newsreels shot *circa* 1920 by Derek Shannon, Cheetham's successor at the Rhyl cinema. They covered such topics as the town's Peace Day celebrations, its Flying Week and its Lifeboat Day and May Day processions. Their titles credited the 'Shannon Film Company' with their production in the form of the monogram 'S. F. Co.'.

Eric Foulkes told me that he had screened some of these

films locally in aid of charity and explained gravely: 'I kept a bucket of water and a bucket of sand ready in case of fire'. In hindsight, and now being only too aware of the potential danger of handling early films, I hate to think what might have happened had there been a fire!

When I first met Eric Foulkes he had already sent Cheetham and Shannon films to the National Film Archive in London for conservation and later return. The Merrie Men films he gave me proved to be a valuable educational resource. My application to the Schools Council for a grant to conserve them was successful, and my colleague Simon Collinge of the then North-East Wales Institute of Further Education took them to a London film laboratory to be copied onto modern 16mm safety film as a not-for-projection 'master'. Rhyl Rotary Club kindly financed a 'show' copy.

However, while preparing Rhyl material for inclusion in the *'Britain on Film' BFI Player* facility in 2016, Mark Davies of the National Screen and Sound Archive of Wales realised that there were two versions of Cheetham's Merrie Men films, having noticed tell-tale differences. They may have been shot as a 'belt-and-braces' exercise to ensure that there was material for screening at the Town Hall four days later. The version that Eric Foulkes gave me is available on *'Britain on Film' BFI Player*; the other one can be seen on *Screenonline: 1890s Films*.

It was also Mark Davies who recognised the 1908 railway film as being from Eric Foulkes's collection by deciphering the sign on the front of the engine.

Eric Foulkes had sent less than two minutes of the 'British' and 'National' schools films to the NFA. But he would occasionally deliver extra footage to me at the teachers' centre. It included the Christ Church boy who looks the camera in the lens, the 'strong horse' game and young Adelaide's Uncle John.

Some years later, Rhyl Town Council and the then Clwyd County Record Office jointly financed their conservation. Their total duration came to over 11 minutes, and can be viewed on the 'Britain on Film' BFI Player.

My second 'lucky dip' resulted from the period I spent at Aberystwyth studying for a higher university degree in 1976-77. In a casual conversation with my landlady Mrs Dilys Gravelle, I mentioned my interest in Cheetham. 'Arthur Cheetham!' she exclaimed knowingly, being well aware of his long association with the town. She suggested a visit to Mr and Mrs Millichamp, an elderly couple who lived near the harbour and who had worked at his Aberystwyth cinema. They advised me to contact their friend Mrs Jerman, widow of a National Library official, who had moved from Aberystwyth to Kerry, near Newtown in Powys. I phoned her, and she gave me details of Cheetham's daughter, Mrs Cordery. My fruitful discussion with her about her father's varied commercial interests is dealt with at length elsewhere in this publication. But she also suggested that a visit to the Chester home of her nephew Stanley Cheetham might be 'of interest'.

'Of interest' proved to be an understatement. Particularly when, during my ensuing visit, he went upstairs to retrieve a large case from under the bed. It was crammed full of film. Sadly, thousands of feet of one large reel had turned into a solid, sticky mass and had to be burned in the garden. But shorter lengths featuring a steamship approaching a landing-stage, children playing on a beach, a football match and a lively street-scene appeared promising.

With the aid of a magnifying-glass I gazed at several frames of the steamship film, read the word 'Munster' and realised that I was looking at *Arrival of the Irish Mail Boat at Holyhead*, since the *Record and Advertiser*'s report of the its first Rhyl screening had mentioned the vessel's name. It was in negative form, as loaded into the camera to capture 'all the movements of the boat as she made for the stage to the lowering of the gangway' in early 1898.

Although J.W. Jones mentions the *Munster* film in his *Rhyl, the Town and its People*, he had never seen it. It was eventually delivered on my behalf by Rhyl Town Council to the NFA, and once I had been provided with a 16mm copy I gave the esteemed local historian a personal screening at his Rhyl retirement home. His appreciative response was: 'It **is** clear, isn't it?' I felt privileged that, after reading and writing about this film, he was at long last able to view it.

But to revert to my visit to Stanley Cheetham's home. My excitement knew no bounds when I studied the film of children on a beach (also in negative form). Could this be his grandfather's very first effort, taken in January 1898 and so condescendingly described by the *Record and Advertiser* as '(considering it was a first attempt) a grand success'? Sadly not. Careful examination by my wife later persuaded me that the children were too lightly clad for January. It was, of course, 'children paddling on Rhyl Sands', first screened at Cheetham's 1899 benefit concert.

As to the football film: my tentative conclusion that it featured the Blackburn Rovers v West Bromwich Albion game of September 1898 was later confirmed by correspondence with Robin Whalley (as acknowledged in a footnote to Chapter 4). I deposited it with the North-West Film Archive, who later included it in a montage prepared for them by Granada TV to introduce the archival film programmes they screen throughout their region in the hope that audience members might have films worthy of conservation in their possession. It was also one of the nine films in the NFA's 1993 touring compilation *Football Shorts: A Celebration of Football History*. But it finally 'came home' during the film centenary celebrations of the late 1990s, when it was screened by the Blackburn Local History Society on the 98th anniversary of the game. Although Promio's *Football* of 1897 is acknowledged to be the oldest surviving football film, Cheetham's *Blackburn Rovers v West Bromwich Albion* remains the oldest one of a competitive game (as confirmed by film historian Luke McKernan's on-line *Filming football « The Bioscope*).

The street-scene film featured a market trader. As he turns to give directions to a visitor, a gang of unruly boys upturn his two-wheeled cart. Among the watching crowd is an apron-clad barmaid in the doorway of the White Lion Spirit Vaults across the road, and a bearded gentleman near the music shop next door steps forward to get a better view. The boys manhandle the cart to and fro, return it to its rightful place *sans* produce and are chased off by the irate owner. This film appears to be by Cheetham: it was in his grandson's collection together with others acknowledged to be his and was (like the *Munster* and the beach films) in negative form. But the location remains a mystery. Extensive study of 19th century trades directories has so far failed to yield any record of a street containing both a White Lion Spirit Vaults and a music shop. A detailed analysis of the boys' movements by David Berry suggests choreography. So, if this film is by Cheetham, it reveals him to be more than a mere recorder of scenes and events in his early days. It was also delivered to the NFA by Rhyl Town Council on my behalf.

Stanley Cheetham's case yielded the 1920s Aberystwyth

films mentioned in Chapter 15. They were later collected by local historian Mrs Margaret Evans and her journalist husband Tom and deposited at the National Library (but now held at the National Screen and Sound Archive, part of that institution). The 'coll v town' film is not the only surviving one to feature Rhyl's pioneer film-maker. Grandson Stanley had safeguarded the original negative of *Marriage of Mr. Gustavus.A.Cheetham Manager of the Central Cinema,Rhyl, to Miss Edith.M. Lawson At Rhyl,Sept 22ND, 1913.* and a 'show' copy which had been screened at numerous family events over the years. Not only does this film record the first day of his parents' life together, but it also features his grandfather, showered with confetti and resplendent in morning suit and top hat, leaving the church with his wife on his arm and chatting later with other guests as they wait for a group photograph. Its conservation was eventually financed jointly by Rhyl Town Council and Clwyd County Record Office.

Mr and Mrs Cheetham Sr must also have featured in the film taken after Bernard's wedding in 1914. The *Cambrian News* reported that it had been screened at the Aberystwyth cinema for three nights during the following week, but it has not survived.

Also in Stanley Cheetham's case was a *circa* 1935 reprint of the 1899 *Royal Visit to Conway* film. It boasted a stylish three-part title sequence providing full details of the event and referring to his grandfather as 'The Pioneer of Moving Pictures in North Wales', 'THEN OF RHYL' and 'Now resident at The Circuit Withington, Manchester'. But I did not need to entrust it to the NFA, since correspondence with them confirmed that a copy had already been deposited from the collection of the late William Jeapes of *Topical Budget* fame.

Had I not been directed to Stanley Cheetham's home through

the good offices of Mrs Gravelle, Mr and Mrs Millichamp, Mrs Jerman and Mrs Cordery, three of his grandfather's films, one possibly shot by him and two featuring him might never again have seen the light of day. If my discovery of these films was fortuitous, their survival is truly amazing. When, as Stanley related, the Aberystwyth cinema burned down in 1935 they were all stored in a metal chest kept in the flat at the rear of the building and were retrieved undamaged. He eventually removed them from the home his father and his Uncle Bernard had shared on the outskirts of Rhyl during their later years, a mere quarter of a mile from where I lived at the time, unaware of the existence of both films and brothers. What if ... ?

Thus ends the lengthy story of safe-keeping, coincidence and co-operation represented by David Berry's 'dusty cans' image – unless more Cheetham footage comes to light. When I first met Stanley Cheetham, he was not much enamoured of the films he had unwittingly saved for posterity. After all, as he observed dispassionately, they were 'old'. But after realising their significance, he began to show an interest in them, recorded his recollections for me and agreed to unveil the plaque at Rhyl Town Hall in his forebear's honour – albeit mischievously maintaining an initial anonymity on the day, thereby causing no little concern to the organizers. But he certainly enjoyed the programme of Cheetham films I then presented to an appreciative audience at the pioneer's favourite Rhyl venue, suitably accompanied on the piano by educationist, musician and broadcaster Rhys Jones.

In retrospect, perhaps David Berry's depiction of Arthur Cheetham's legacy might well have read: 'two separate collections of films in dusty cans **and a battered suitcase**'.

Films mentioned in this chapter which can be viewed on 'Britain on Film' BFI Player: *Peace Day Celebrations at Rhyl*; *Flying Week at Rhyl*; *Life Boat Day at Rhyl* and *Rhyl May Day* [not to be confused with Cheetham's *May Day Procession 1903*] (all by the Shannon Film Company) and *Wedding* [replacing the original '*Marriage*'] *of G.A. Cheetham and Miss E.M. Lawson* (camera operator unknown)

Filmography

This list establishes, as far as possible, the dates when Cheetham's films were shot, mainly by reference to previews, advertisements and reports on his film-shows in the *Rhyl Journal* (abbreviated to *RJ*) and the *Rhyl Record and Advertiser* (abbreviated to *RR&A*). Also listed are five others: one attributable to him, one possibly shot by him, two featuring him and one presumably featuring him. Those films which have survived in part or *in toto* are identified as such

1898

1. Rhyl Sands: *RR&A*, 22 January, p. [5] (report on its screening, Thursday 13 January: 'taken only the preceding Friday', i.e. 7 January)

NB: nos **2** to **14** below were shot on various dates after the screening of **Rhyl Sands:** *RR&A*, 26 March, p. [4]; *RJ*, 26 March, p. [7] and 2 April, p. [4] (advertisements and report on their first screening, Monday 28 March)

2, 3 and **4. Rhyl Station representing the passing through of the Irish Mail, the special engine and coach of the District Superintendent, and the steaming into the station of the 12.50 train**

5. Loading Slates at Portmadoc

6. Arrival of Irish Mail Boat at Holyhead
Survives

7. Horse Fair at Llangollen

8. Ladies Boating at Aberystwyth

9. Football Match at Rhyl (shot March 12th): Town v. Amateurs

10. Arrival of Train at Llanrwst

11. Street Scene in High Street, Wrexham

12. A Diver at Work at Holyhead

13. Rough Sea at Rhyl (shot Thursday, March 24th)

14. an express train catching mail bags

15. a splendid view of the May-Day Procession: *RJ*, 21 May, p. [7] (report on a private screening 'last evening', i.e. Thursday 19 May). **NB:** Rhyl papers dated Saturday were then published on a Friday, as explained in Chapter 4
Also **Annual May Day Demonstration! Monday May 2nd:** *RJ*, 23 April, p. [7] (advertisement dating the event)

16. in Queen-street last week when the steam roller was at work: *RJ*, 21 May, p. [7] (report on a private screening, Thursday 19 May, dating the film to the week commencing Monday 16 May)

NB: nos **17, 18** and **19** below: *RR&A* (*List of Visitors*), 2 July, p. [3] (preview of their first Rhyl screening, Thursday 7 July)

17. A picture of Colwyn Bay beach, showing the niggers performing

18. the crowd leaving the Happy Valley at Llandudno

19. A scene in Penmaenmawr Station
Also described in more detail as **a train arriving and departing in Penmaenmawr Station:** *RR&A* (*List of Visitors*), 20 August, p. [3] (preview of a later Rhyl screening, Monday 22 August)

20. a reproduction of the Blackburn Rovers v West Bromwich Albion football match played at Ewood Park on September 24th: *Northern Daily Telegraph*, 19 October, p. 3 (advertisement for its first Blackburn screening, Wednesday 19 October, dating the match)
A fragment survives

1899

21. Royal Visit to Conway and its Historic Castle on May 5th 1899: from the three-part title of a *circa* 1935 reprint, dating the event
Survives

22, 23. both taken on the 26th inst. ... well-known double dance [and] that popular nigger sketch entitled "The School": *RJ*, 5 August, p. [2] (report on their first and second Rhyl screenings, Monday and Tuesday, 31 July and 1 August, dating them to Wednesday 26 July)
Two versions of each film survive (as explained in Chapter 16)

24. the crowd leaving the Niggers' entertainment on Wednesday afternoon: *RJ*, 2 September, p. [2] (preview of its first Rhyl screening, Monday 4 September, dating it to Wednesday 30 August)

25. taken this week ... of children paddling on Rhyl Sands: *RJ*, 2 September, p. [2] (preview of its first Rhyl screening, Monday 4 September, dating it to the week commencing Monday 28 August)
Survives

1902

26. New Local Pictures: *RJ*, 11 January, p. [7] (advertisement for the first two Rhyl screenings of unidentified footage, Tuesday and Wednesday, 14 and 15 January)

27. ROYAL VISIT TO RHYL: *RR&A*, 17 May, p [4] and 24 May, p. [4] (advertisements for its screening throughout Whit-week, 19-24 May, dating the event to Monday 12 May)

28. Children leaving the National Schools on Tuesday last: *RR&A*, 24 May, p. [4] (advertisement for its screening on Thursday, Friday and Saturday of Whit-week, 22-24 May, dating it to Tuesday 13 May)
Survives

29. Children leaving Christ Church Schools, taken last Friday: *RR&A*, 24 May, p. [4] (advertisement for its screening on Thursday, Friday and Saturday of Whit-week, 22-24 May, dating it to Friday 16 May)
Survives

30. A Crowd on Rhyl Parade: *RR&A*, 24 May, p. [4] (advertisement for the screening of unidentified footage on Thursday, Friday and Saturday of Whit-week, 22-24 May)

1903

31. The 1903 May Day Procession in Rhyl: *RJ*, 30 May, p. [7] (advertisement for its Whit Monday, Tuesday and Wednesday, 1, 2 and 3 June screening)
Also **May-Day Carnival at Rhyl:** *RR&A*, 2 May, p. [8] (report on the event, dating it to Thursday, 30 April)
Survives

32. The Visit of "Buffalo Bill", May 27: *RJ*, 30 May, p. [7] (advertisement for its Whit Monday, Tuesday and Wednesday, 1, 2 and 3 June screening, dating the event)
Survives

33. scenes … at Nant Hall, Prestatyn, in connection with the Rhyl Cycling Club's Outing: *RJ*, 6 June, p. [2] (report on its Whit Monday, Tuesday and Wednesday, 1, 2 and 3 June screening)
Also **CYCLING CLUB PICNIC. – on Thursday week:** *RR&A*, 6 June, p. [8] (report on the event, dating it to Thursday 28 May)
A fragment survives

34. The "Gorsedd" at Rhyl: *RJ*, 26 September, p. [7] (advertisement for its screening throughout the week commencing Monday 28 September)
Also **PROCLAMATION OF THE ROYAL NATIONAL EISTEDDFOD OF WALES:** *RR&A*, 8 August 1903, p. [3] (report on the event, dating it to Friday 31 July)

1904

35. an Unique set of Silvograph Copyright Pictures (only just taken) of Slate Quarrying in North Wales: *RR&A*, 21 May, p. [4] (advertisement for its screening throughout Whit-week, commencing Monday 23 May)

36. Local Pictures taken in Rhyl this week: *RR&A*, 21 May, p. [4] (advertisement for the screening of unidentified footage throughout Whit-week, commencing Monday 23 May, and dating the film to the week commencing Monday 16 May)

1907

37. A Signboard Comedy [Cheetham's dispute with the local council]: *RJ*, 29 June, p. [4] (report on the filming of the workmen attempting to remove the projecting signboard, dating that part of the film to Thursday 27 June)
the audience dispersing after last Saturday afternoon's entertainment: *RJ*, 6 July, p. [4] (report on the filming of the second sequence, dating it to Saturday, 29 June)
NB: no local newspaper reference to **the third sequence**, showing Cheetham's employee pasting the poster onto the cinema wall
Survives as a series of selected 'stills' (as explained in Chapter 16)

38. TERRIBLE FIRE IN RHYL [Queen's Palace fire]: *RR&A*, 30 November, p. [6] (report on the event, dating it to Sunday 24 November)
Also **On Tuesday night Mr Cheetham put on a most realistic film of the fire:** *RJ*, 30 November, p. [4] (report on 26 November screening)

the addition of the fire call taken last Saturday: *RJ*, 14 December, p. [6] (report on the screening throughout the week commencing Monday 9 December and dating the 'addition' to Saturday 7 December)

an animated portrait picture of the Brigade ... as a finale: *Programme. SILVOGRAPH ANIMATED PICTURES. CENTRAL HALL, Market Street, Rhyl.* [1908], p. [17] (also indicates final order of sequences)

1908

39. at the Central Hall ... this week ... a picture taken last Thursday of the new Pavilion works: *RJ*, 28 March, p. [6] (report on screening throughout the week commencing Monday 23 March and dating the film to Thursday 19 March)

40. the ceremony of the laying of the foundation stones of the new Pavilion, which took place yesterday: *RJ*, 28 March, p. [4] (report on the event, dating it to Thursday 26 March)
Also **will be put on for the first time on Monday next (April 6th):** *RJ*, 4 April, p. [4] (preview of first screening)

41. Among the pictures ... the recent May Day Procession: *RJ*, 6 June, p. [4] (preview of screening throughout Whit-week, commencing Monday, 8 June)
Also **RHYL MAY Festivities. THURSDAY, MAY 7th:** *RJ*, 2 May, p. [5] (advertisement, dating the event)

42. Sunny Rhyl First Stop: *RJ*, 25 July, p. [9] (report on event and film, dating both to Friday 17 July)
Survives

1909

43. A Motor Mystery: *RJ*, 30 January, p. [4] (report on screening throughout the week commencing Monday 25 January)
Also **A MOTOR MYSTERY:** *The Rhyl and North Wales Weekly News*, 16 February 1912, p. 1 (advertisement for Cheetham's Colwyn Bay cinema, confirming the filming of the 'accident' at Penmaen-bach headland)

1911

44. his reproduction of the Rhyl May Day procession: *RJ*, 13 May, p. [4] (report on its screening throughout the week commencing Monday 8 May)
Also **Rhyl May Day Festivities, Thursday, May 4th 1911:** *RJ*, 29 April, p. [2] (advertisement dating the event)

45. a cinematic picture of the Royal visit of Saturday last … shown to an audience on Monday night: *RJ*, 22 July, p. [4] (dating the event to Saturday 15 July and its first Aberystwyth screening to Monday 17 July)
Survives, at least in part, if it is the Pathé-distributed **Aberystwyth. The King and Queen Accompanied by the Prince of Wales and Princess Mary Perform a Stone-laying Ceremony** (as suggested in Chapter 13)

46. For some weeks … engaged in taking a series of cinematograph pictures for the Aberystwyth Corporation, for the purpose of advertising the town: *RJ*, 30 September, p. [4]

1912

47. The Animated Picture of VIVIAN HEWITT'S FLIGHT TO IRELAND: handbill printed by Cheetham and reproduced in *Modest Millionaire* (below)
Also **William Hywel.** *Modest Millionaire*, p. 70 (dating the event to Friday 26 April) and pp. 75-6 (describing the film)

ATTRIBUTABLE TO CHEETHAM

48. [boys upset market trader's cart]: explanation in Chapter 16
Survives

POSSIBLY BY CHEETHAM

49. showing this week the damage done to the Promenade during the late storm: *Cambrian News and Merionethshire Standard*, 30 December 1910, p. 8 (dating the first Aberystwyth screening to the week commencing Monday 26 December)

FEATURING CHEETHAM

50. Marriage of Mr. Gustavus. A. Cheetham Manager of the Central Cinema, Rhyl, to Miss Edith. M. Lawson At Rhyl, Sept 22ND, 1913: title, dating the event
Survives

51. First Road Race. Coll v Town, Inaugurating the Aberystwyth Town Harriers 1929 (shot by Gustavus Cheetham)
Survives

PRESUMABLY FEATURING CHEETHAM

52. POPULAR WEDDING [of his son Bernard] **AT ST MICHAELS:** *Cambrian News and Merionethshire Standard,* 1 May 1914, p. 6 (dating the event to Monday 27 April)

Also **MR CHEETHAM'S CINEMA, MARKET STREET:** *Cambrian News and Merionethshire Standard,* 8 May 1914, p. 8 (dating its Aberystwyth screening to 'the early part of the week', commencing Monday 4 May)

Further Suggested Reading and Viewing

The following print-based and on-line resources have proved invaluable in the preparation of this book. I hope that they, together with the films listed at the end of most chapters, will offer opportunities for the further study and enjoyment of early cinema

GENERAL

IMDb [International Media Database]. On-line. A veritable mine of information about films and film-makers

Stephen Herbert and Luke McKernan, eds. *Who's Who of Victorian Cinema*. An on-line guide to over 300 leading figures, from the first glimmerings in the 1870s to the death of Queen Victoria in January 1901

Stephen Herbert, compiler. *When the Movies Began: a chronology of the world's earliest film productions and film-shows.* Part of *Who's Who of Victorian Cinema*

Silent Era: Progressive Silent Film List. On-line. Its lengthy alphabetical list leads to detailed information about hundreds of titles

THE UK

John Barnes. *The Beginnings of the Cinema in England 1894–1901*, vols 1-5 (1894–96, 1897, 1898, 1899 and 1900 respectively). A major contribution to the study of early UK film. Detailed treatment of individuals in the text and extensive quotations from catalogues and trade periodicals in the filmographies. The 1899 volume lists most of Cheetham's 1898 and 1899 output

David Berry. *Wales and Cinema, the First Hundred Years*. A labour of love in over 400 illustrated and annotated pages. Includes a chronology of 'Film Milestones' and the film and TV credits of 40 Welsh actors, directors and editors. Seven pages are devoted to Cheetham. Offered modestly as 'the work of an enthusiastic film critic and writer rather than a professional historian'

Denis Gifford. *The British Film Catalogue Volume 1 Fiction Film, 1895–1994* and *The British Film Catalogue Volume 2 Non-Fiction Film, 1888–1994*. Annual lists of films, described in considerably less detail than by Barnes but covering a much longer period. The non-fiction volume lists most of Cheetham's 1898 and 1899 output, together with the 1902 'British' and 'National' schools films (wrongly dated to 1900) and *Fire at Palace, Rhyl* (1907) advertised in the *Kinematograph Weekly*

Cecil M. Hepworth. *Came the Dawn, Memories of a Film Pioneer*. The entertaining autobiography of an early film producer

Rachael Low and Roger Manvell. *The History of the British Film, volume 1: 1896–1906* and Rachael Low. *The History of the British Film, volume 2: 1906–1914*. Apart from the *genre* classification in volume 1 (for which examples are provided)

both volumes cover much the same field as Barnes, but over a longer period

Vanessa Toulmin. *Electric Edwardians, The Story of the Mitchell & Kenyon Collection.* The films of the Blackburn pioneers, advertised as 'local films for local people'. Themes such as Leisure and Recreation, Sport, Industry and the Boer War are placed in their social context

Peter Yorke. *William Haggar (1851–1925) fairground film-maker.* Draws on oral reminiscences, unpublished family memories and contemporary press reports about the author's great-grandfather. Includes a chronology of films produced between 1901 and 1915

Welsh Newspapers Online. While public libraries and county record offices are the traditional repositories of local newspapers (whether as hard copies or on microfilm), this service is offered free of charge by the National Library of Wales. It provides access to a wide range of local and national papers, generally up to 1900. Extensive use has been made of it during the preparation of this book, especially the *Rhyl Journal* and the *Rhyl Record and Advertiser* (both available up to 1910) and the *Cambrian News* (available up to 1919, but excluding 1911–1913)

THE USA

AFI [the American Film Institute] *Catalog of Feature Films.* On-line. Detailed information on cast, crew, plot summaries, subjects, *genre* and historical notes are included for US films from 1893 onwards

Inventing Entertainment – Library of Congress. On-line. Edison's films and sound recordings from 1891 to 1904 are listed. The films (described on pp. 1-13) can be viewed, including some from Kinetoscope days and others mentioned in this book. Select 'Collection Items', then 'Sort By' for title or year

Charles Musser. *Before the Nickelodeon. Edwin S. Porter and the Edison Manufacturing Company*. In spite of this book's title, Porter and the Edison Company are placed in a wider context in the history of early film. An edited version can be studied on-line

FRANCE

The Lumières

Catalogue Lumière, L'œuvre cinématographique des frères Lumière. On-line. Its timeline lists, describes (in French only, to date) 1,428 films shot between 1895 and 1905 and illustrates them with 'stills'

Les Frères Lumière – Liste de 61 films, SensCritique. On-line. Mainly 'stills' from a selection of actualities, interest films, topicals, dramas and comedies, one animation and a music-hall act, all shot between 1895 and 1899. 13 of them can be viewed in their entirety (some with modern musical accompaniment). Countries visited to produce interest and topical films include Azerbaijan, China, Egypt and Italy

Films Lumière 1-12 features 365 films which can be viewed on *YouTube*. No. 12 has been referred to at the end of Chapter 10 in connection with *Le repas fantastique*. One user's comment on reaching no. 12 was 'It's been over 6 hours of these and still haven't seen every Lumiere film available in this collection'

Méliès

Elizabeth Ezra. *French Film Directors: Georges Méliès The birth of the* auteur. A biography of a pioneer who directed, edited, produced, designed and starred in over 500 films between 1896 and 1913

Hugo. This 126-minute film of 2011, available on DVD, is a seamless blend of fact (sometimes interpreted creatively) and fiction set in *circa* 1930 Paris. Ben Kingsley stars as the elderly Méliès. Flashbacks include magic at *Théâtre Robert-Houdin* and filming at Méliès's 'glasshouse' studio

Internet Archive – The Georges Méliès Collection. On-line. 71 films (including some mentioned in this book) can be viewed, together with synopses. Trick-photography abounds, and some films have modern musical accompaniments

Pathé

Richard Abel. *The Ciné Goes to Town: French Cinema, 1896–1914.* Includes the period when *Société Pathé Frères* were the world's major film producers and distributors

Fondation Jérôme Seydoux-Pathé. Filmographie Pathé. On-line. Year-by-year lists of films from 1896 onwards, complete with *résumés* (synopses) and other details (nearly all in French)

Acknowledgements

I gratefully acknowledge the help, advice and support received from numerous individuals and institutions during the years spent researching and compiling this book. The late David Berry, to whose memory it is dedicated, was a constant source of inspiration. His insistence that I publish my research into Cheetham was tempered with the advice of a seasoned journalist to 'keep the narrative going'. I hope that he would have been pleased with the result

My interviews with Mrs Gwen Cordery, Mrs Adelaide Clarke, Mr Albert Edwards and the film-maker's grandson Stanley Cheetham give this book a dimension way beyond bare facts gleaned from conventional sources. Sadly, they are no longer with us, but their words live on in the sound-tapes deposited at the National Screen and Sound Archive of Wales

Newspapers in microfilm and hard-copy form, books and facilities for viewing films on *BFI Screenonline* were made available variously by Caerffili County Library Service, including Caerffili Branch Library; Cardiff Central Library; Colwyn Bay Library; Flintshire County Library Service, including its @nswers/@tebion Centre and Mold Branch Library; Hammersmith and Fulham Borough Library Service, including Hammersmith Central Library; Rhyl Library, Museum & Arts Centre; Wrexham Central Library; the Cardiff ATRiuM Centre and the Newport School of Creative and Cultural Industries of the University of South Wales; Denbighshire, Flintshire and Wrexham County Record Offices

Thanks are also due to the following individuals for their help and advice in various ways: Iola Baines, Mark Davies and their ever-obliging colleagues at the National Screen and Sound Archive of Wales; the late John Barnes; Peter Bidmead and his wife Maureen, related to Cheetham through the film-maker's mother; film historian Christopher Draper; Dr E.M. Erin; Charles Evans-Günther and David Jones, former colleagues at the Clwyd Centre for Educational Technology; David Eve; Tony Fletcher, film researcher at the Cinema Museum; David Johnson, late of Meggitt PLC; Luke McKernan, Lead Curator, News and Moving Image at the British Library; Ian Meyrick; Professor Charles Musser of Yale University; the National Library of Wales; James Offer; the late John K. Parker; Robin Whalley; Alison Wilson; Dr Goronwy Wynne and the late A.G. Veysey, Chief Archivist of the former Clwyd County Council

My wife listened, read and offered constructive comments as the book took shape, not least her astute observation regarding Cheetham's 1899 beach film. Diolch o galon, Lisa

And finally, to Myrddin ap Dafydd and his colleagues at Gwasg Carreg Gwalch, in particular graphic artist Eleri Owen and compositor Dwynwen Williams: my appreciation of their care and attention.